Using Accounting Information:
An Interactive Learning Approach

Linda Plunkett
The University of Charleston, S.C.

Larry Walther
The University of Texas–Arlington

Lanny Solomon
The University of Texas–Arlington

West Publishing Company
Minneapolis/St. Paul   New York   Los Angeles   San Francisco

West's Commitment to the Environment
In 1906, West Publishing Company began recycling materials left over from the production of books. This began a tradition of efficient and responsible use of resources. Today, up to 95 percent of our legal books and 70 percent of our college and school texts are printed on recycled, acid-free stock. West also recycles nearly 22 million pounds of scrap paper annually—the equivalent of 181,717 trees. Since the 1960s, West has devised ways to capture and recycle waste inks, solvents, oils, and vapors created in the printing process. We also recycle plastics of all kinds, wood, glass, corrugated cardboard, and batteries, and have eliminated the use of styrofoam book packaging. We at West are proud of the longevity and the scope of our commitment to the environment.

Production, Prepress, Printing and Binding by West Publishing Company.

Contents

■ PART 3   Role Plays, Simulations, and Field Studies   107

■ PART 4   Innovative Challenges   149

Notes to Students

You will quickly discover that this book is totally unlike your traditional accounting textbook. Although the material contained in these pages can be considered "accounting," the presentation and the use of the exercises are unique. Some items here are called cases and will be used for class discussions. Some assignments are related to straight-forward research. Some involve reading and analyzing articles. Role plays, simulations of real-life situations, and field studies are also included. You will even find games and other entertaining exercises.

All of the assignments have multiple purposes. Primarily, they will stimulate your comprehension of accounting subjects in the contexts of business and your life. You will learn to use accounting information to make decisions. The exercises will also enhance your oral and written communication skills. Some of these projects will involve working in groups, so you will have opportunities to interact meaningfully with your classmates and instructor. All of these benefits will ultimately help you in your career.

When you work the exercises in this book, you will become an active participant in the learning process rather than a passive recipient of information. You may experience a degree of frustration at first as you learn to work with the unstructured scenarios presented in many of the exercises. The cases, for example, have no "correct" or absolute solutions. Unlike the problems at the end of your textbook chapters, there are no check figures. In other words, the numerical components of the assignments are not the target of the exercise. Even though some cases will require computations or schedules, the major purpose of each is the development of your analytical skills and your ability to assess situations critically. You will need to make assumptions and think creatively. Further, you will learn to communicate your conclusions concisely, whether in an oral or a written presentation. These skills require practice, but you should feel at ease after a few exercises.

As you become more proficient in decision making, you will also find that your ability to express your ideas becomes refined. Regardless of the structure of an assigned project, it is imperative that you be an dynamic participant in the process. Speak out, speak clearly, and speak often.

In order to have fruitful class discussions, you will be expected to:

1. Be prepared for every exercise.
2. Contribute your ideas, opinions, and questions in each case.
3. Critically evaluate each assignment.
4. Be considerate and tolerant of others' opinions.
5. Be thoughtful and prompt.

The overriding point of this book is to present innovative ways to learn and understand accounting principles. An often-quoted Chinese proverb goes something like this:

I hear and I forget;
I see and I remember;
I do and I understand.

We have created the exercises in this book so that you will "do and understand."

We would like to thank several individuals who were especially helpful in creating this book. William Stahlin at Drexel University kindly allowed us to expand his trivia game for this book. Roger Daniels of the University of Charleston, S.C. wrote the cases, "Accounting Practice: Seven Centuries of Evolution" and "Coca-Cola, Then and Now." Wanda DeLeo at Winthrop University recounted her experiences in the project, "An Accounting Journal for Students." Jerry Fewox at Trident Technical College wrote, "Bulldog Enterprises." Julie Poteet designed the crossword puzzles. Janine Wilson and Bob Horan at West Publishing gave invaluable publishing assistance.

Most of all, we would like to thank our students over the years who gave us the opportunities and inspiration that we used to develop most of these exercises. We would like to hear your suggestions and feedback, too. We welcome the opportunity for your contribution. Most of all, we hope that you will have fun in accounting.

Linda Plunkett
Larry Walther
Lanny Solomon

PART 1

Decision Cases
for
Active Learning

Accounting Practice: Seven Centuries of Evolution

■ INTRODUCTION

The accounting profession is rich in history. Many of the currently accepted practices of the profession can be traced to northern Italy during the Renaissance period. Luca Pacioli, an Italian monk, who was a mathematician and friend of Leonardo da Vinci, is credited with first formally proposing the double-entry system that forms the cornerstone of modern accounting practice. Pacioli describes the double-entry system in his work, *Summa de Arithmetica, Geometria, Proportioni, et Proportionalita*, published in 1494. This landmark piece describes a system of journals, ledgers, and transactions. The transactions collected and described in these books of entry form the basis for the preparation of the balance sheet and income statement (initially called the statement of profit and loss).

Even before the influence of Pacioli, merchants on the European continent kept books describing their daily business activities. These records clearly indicate that accounting systems much like those of today existed during the Middle Ages. A recently discovered set of 14th century accounting records and financial statements provide many insights into the evolution of accounting practice. The 1399 financial statements of Francesco di Marco Datini and Company, a Barcelona merchant, is a classic example of accounting practice during the Middle Ages.[1] The financial statements indicate that many of the current theories inherent in modern accounting practice existed to some degree during the Middle Ages.

The Datini financial statements provide a glimpse of one important aspect of medieval society. Commerce was a centerpiece of medieval culture and the accounting records provide historians with many vital pieces of information about this period of time. The Datini balance sheet and profit and loss statement included the following accounts:

---

[1] Philip Piaker, "The Use of Medieval Statements for Teaching Accounting," *The Accounting Review* (July 1972), pp. 609–610.

Francesco di Marco Datini and Co. in Barcelona
Balance Sheet on January 1, 1399

Assets

Cash
Receivables
Balances with foreign correspondents
Datini branches in other places
Inventories
Fixtures—office furniture
Fixtures—Martha, our slave
Miscellaneous
Bad debts
Untraced error in casting the balance
   Total

Liabilities

Payables
Balance with foreign correspondents
Datini branches in other places
Consignment sales
Reserve for accrued taxes and contingencies
Owner's equity
   Total

Francesco di Marco Datini and Co. in Barcelona
Statement of Profit and Loss
July 11, 1397–January 31, 1399

Profits on trade
Profits on foreign exchange
Credit balance of merchandise expense
   Total

Deduct expenses
   Rent for eighteen months
   Irrecoverable account
   Convoy expense
   Living expenses
   Depreciation and office equipment
   Reserve for unpaid taxes and other accruals
      Total expenses

   Net income (to balance sheet)

While it is apparent that many of the accounts found in the Datini financial statements reflect medieval society, the basic structure of the statements is quite similar to that of modern financial statements. The Datini statements reflect that owner's equity was well developed at this time. Net income is calculated and becomes a part of owner's equity on the balance sheet. This "articulation" is a fundamental concept of modern financial accounting.

The statement of profit and loss does not include interest as either a revenue or expense. This omission is due to the religious and political prohibitions against charging interest. The medieval period is marked by a negative view of *usury*, or the charging of interest. The treatment of interest is just one example of how modern financial statements differ from those of centuries passed. The Datini statements are valuable artifacts, providing insight into the evolution of accounting practice.

■ DIRECTIONS

1. Using the specific account titles of the Datini statements, identify and briefly explain how these early statements are like those of today with respect to:
   a. Accrual accounting
   b. Matching principle
   c. Double-entry system
2. How do the Datini statements differ with respect to the periodicity assumption?
3. Although several types of expense accounts are presented in the Datini statements, there is no record of insurance expense or advertising expense. Why do you think that these expenses do not appear? Briefly explain.
4. It has been argued that accounting is reflective of a particular society. In other words, the Datini financial statements may provide clues about medieval social values. Which single balance sheet account is most indicative of the social values and structure of medieval society?

Coca-Cola, Then and Now

■ INTRODUCTION

The Coca-Cola Company has emerged as America's leading soft-drink business. The 1991 annual report of The Coca-Cola Company highlights the fact that it is the sixth-largest U.S. company, with a market value in excess of $53 billion. Coca-Cola has survived and prospered for over a century by keeping soft-drink bottling as its primary line of business. The financial statements of Coke provide a window for studying the evolution of financial reporting in the United States.

When Coca-Cola was established in 1886, there were virtually no standards for reporting the revenues, expenses, assets, liabilities, and equity accounts of firms doing business in the United States. The inherent lack of standards caused a great deal of inconsistency in what information was reported to interested parties. In many instances, no information was reported outside the company. Potential investors, creditors, and others were unable to obtain the vital information needed to make decisions regarding purchasing the company's stock or extending credit. These problems were partially responsible for the stock market crash in 1929, and eventually led to the establishment of uniform financial reporting standards and independentaudit requirements for publicly held companies.

The annual financial statements of The Coca-Cola Company are audited each year by an independent accounting firm. Audit reports (which are really letters included in an annual report) signify to investors, creditors, and other interested parties that a certain level of review of the company was performed. In other words, an audit helps financial statement users decide whether they can rely on the information presented in the financial statements.

It would be almost impossible to check every transaction of a company, because such a review would involve millions of items. Therefore, auditors rely on a statistical sample of transactions when rendering an audit opinion. Thus, only a portion of the transactions of Coca-Cola are audited each year to determine whether the financial statements are fairly presented.

Coca-Cola's 1929 and 1991 balance sheets and audit reports are presented below.[1]

---

[1] Reproduced with permission of The Coca-Cola Company.

CONSOLIDATED CONDENSED BALANCE SHEET

The Coca-Cola Company, Atlanta, Georgia, and Its Subsidiaries

December 31, 1929

ASSETS

CURRENT:

Cash on Deposit	$ 3,508,231.97	
Government Securities—At Cost	3,067,172.95	
Notes Receivable	10,575.51	
Accounts Receivable	1,242,108.78	
Inventory-Merchandise on Hand (Priced at Lower of Cost or Market)	9,136,213.84	$16,964,303.05

INVESTMENT IN COMPANY'S OWN CLASS "A"

STOCK—AT COST	9,433,732.70

OTHER ASSETS:

Investment in Securities of Other Companies	$ 109,860.00	
Sundry Notes and Accounts Receivable	272,107.70	381,967.70

PERMANENT:

Land		$ 1,071,566.25	
Buildings	$4,494,118.50		
Machinery and Equipment	2,930,755.94		
Bottles and Cases	599,066.50		
	$8,023,940.94		
Less: Allowance for Depreciation	2,789,870.31	5,234,070.63	6,305,636.88

FORMULAE, TRADE-MARK AND GOODWILL	21,931,320.52

DEFERRED CHARGES:

Unexpired Insurance and Prepaid Expenses	45,332.27
	$55,062,293.12

LIABILITIES

CURRENT:

Accounts Payable	$ 909,663.51	
Accrued Accounts	30,729.78	$ 940,393.29

RESERVES:

For Current Income Taxes	$ 1,788,239.16	
For Contingencies and Miscellaneous Operations	6,687,451.87	8,475,691.03

NOMINAL

CAPITAL STOCK:

Class "A"—1,000,000 Shares-No Par Value	$ 5,000,000.00	
Common—1,000,000 Shares-No Par Value	25,000,000.00	
	$30,000,000.00	
PROFIT AND LOSS SURPLUS	15,646,208.80	45,646,208.80
		$55,062,293.12

Consolidated Balance Sheets *The Coca-Cola Company and Subsidiaries*

December 31,	1991	1990
(In thousands except share data)		
Assets		
Current		
Cash and cash equivalents	$ 1,058,250	$1,429,555
Marketable securities, at cost (approximates market)	58,946	62,569
	1,117,196	1,492,124
Trade accounts receivable, less allowances of $34,567 in 1991 and $29,510 in 1990	933,448	913,541
Finance subsidiary-receivables	36,172	38,199
Inventories	987,764	982,313
Prepaid expenses and other assets	1,069,664	716,601
Total Current Assets	4,144,244	4,142,778
Investments and Other Assets		
Investments		
Coca-Cola Enterprises Inc. (CCE)	602,776	666,847
Coca-Cola Amatil Limited	570,774	569,057
Other, principally bottling companies	980,465	788,718
Finance subsidiary-receivables	288,471	128,119
Long-term receivables and other assets	442,135	321,977
	2,884,621	2,474,718
Property, Plant and Equipment		
Land	172,781	147,057
Buildings and improvements	1,200,672	1,059,969
Machinery and equipment	2,680,446	2,204,188
Containers	390,737	374,526
	4,444,636	3,785,740
Less allowances for depreciation	1,554,754	1,400,175
	2,889,882	2,385,565
Goodwill and Other Intangible Assets	303,681	275,126
	$10,222,428	$9,278,187

December 31,	1991	1990
Liabilities and Share-Owners' Equity		
Current		
Accounts payable and accrued expenses	**$ 1,914,379**	$1,576,426
Loans and notes payable	**845,823**	1,742,179
Finance subsidiary-notes payable	**346,767**	161,432
Current maturities of long-term debt	**109,707**	97,272
Accrued taxes	**900,884**	719,182
Total Current Liabilities	**4,117,560**	4,296,491
Long-Term Debt	**985,258**	535,861
Other Liabilities	**493,765**	332,060
Deferred Income Taxes	**200,027**	264,611
Share-Owners' Equity		
Preferred stock, $1 par value- Authorized 100,000,000 shares; Issued: 3,000 shares of Cumulative Money Market Preferred Stock in 1991 and 1990; Outstanding: No shares in 1991; 750 shares in 1990, stated at aggregate liquidation preference	**—**	75,000
Common stock, $.50 par value- Authorized: 1,400,000,000 shares; Issued: 843,675,547 shares in 1991; 840,487,486 shares in 1990	**421,838**	420,244
Capital surplus	**639,990**	512,703
Reinvested earnings	**7,425,514**	6,447,576
Unearned compensation related to outstanding restricted stock	**(114,909)**	(67,760)
Foreign currency translation adjustment	**(4,909)**	4,031
	8,367,524	7,391,794
Less treasury stock, at cost (179,195,464 common shares in 1991; 172,248,315 common shares in 1990)	**3,941,706**	3,542,630
	4,425,818	3,849,164
	$10 222,428	$9,278,187

See Notes to Consolidated Financial Statements.

ERNST & ERNST
AUDITS AND SYSTEMS
TAX SERVICE

Atlanta, January 31, 1930.

We Hereby Certify,

That we have audited the books of account and record of THE COCA-COLA COMPANY, Atlanta, Georgia, and its subsidiaries, as at December 31, 1929, and that, based upon our examination and information obtained, it is our opinion that the annexed Consolidated Condensed Balance Sheet is drawn so as to correctly reflect the financial condition of the Companies at the date named, and that the relative Consolidated Statements of Operations, and Profit and Loss-Surplus are correct.

(Signed)   ERNST & ERNST,
Public Accountants
and Auditors.

Report of Independent Auditors

Board of Directors and Share Owners
The Coca-Cola Company

We have audited the accompanying consolidated balance sheets of The Coca-Cola Company and subsidiaries as of December 31, 1991 and 1990, and the related consolidated statements of income, share-owners' equity and cash flows for each of the three years in the period ended December 31, 1991. These financial statements are the responsibility of the Company's management. Our responsibility is to express an opinion on these financial statements based on our audits.

We conducted our audits in accordance with generally accepted auditing standards. Those standards require that we plan and perform the audit to obtain reasonable assurance about whether the financial statements are free of material misstatement. An audit includes examining, on a test basis, evidence supporting the amounts and disclosures in the financial statements. An audit also includes assessing the accounting principles used and significant estimates made by management, as well as evaluating the overall financial statement presentation. We believe that our audits provide a reasonable basis for our opinion.

In our opinion, the financial statements referred to above present fairly, in all material respects, the consolidated financial position of The Coca-Cola Company and subsidiaries at December 31, 1991 and 1990, and the consolidated results of their operations and their cash flows for each of the three years in the period ended December 31, 1991, in conformity with generally accepted accounting principles.

Ernst & Young

Atlanta, Georgia
January 24, 1992

■ DIRECTIONS

1. Compare and contrast the 1929 and 1991 balance sheets of Coca-Cola. (Keep in mind that the 1929 annual report was prepared just after the stock market crash of 1929 and before strict financial reporting requirements were implemented in the 1930s.) Highlight at least five differences between the two statements. What do you believe is the most significant difference? Briefly explain your answer.

2. Suppose that you have been given $100,000 to invest in any common stock and are considering investing the entire amount in Coca-Cola. Which of the balance sheets (1929 or 1991) do you find more useful in making such a decision? Explain the reason for your conclusion.

3. Although both the 1929 and 1991 audit reports of Coca-Cola were issued by the same CPA firm (Ernst and Ernst later became Ernst and Young), the two reports are different in many respects. Specifically, how do each of these reports differ?

The Spaghetti Taco

■ INTRODUCTION

Joel Gray recently created a new fast food—the spaghetti taco. He decided to sell it from streetside vending carts in a major downtown area. Joel started the business on June 1 with a beginning cash investment of $5,000. Eighty percent of the investment was used to buy his first cart, and the rest was kept for cash reserves. Food, supplies, and labor for the month of June totaled $2,000. Joel obtained all of these items on credit, and none had been paid for as of July 1. All sales during June were cash and totaled $4,000.

Joel was delighted with his first month of operations. He calculated a $2,000 net profit, which was quite an impressive return on a $4,000 investment. Joel enthusiastically continued with his plans for expansion by purchasing a second cart on July 1. He planned to buy two more carts in August.

■ DIRECTIONS

Calculate income and cash flow information for Joel's business for June and July. Identify Joel's problem, and explain the paradox created by rapid growth.

Name That Industry

■ **INTRODUCTION**

As you study the basic accounting concepts used in the presentation of financial statements, you start to develop the ability to recognize the nature of the entity for which financial statements are presented. For example, early in your accounting studies you learned to distinguish between the income statement of a manufacturing business and that of a service business. Conversely, you may infer certain financial characteristics that would relate to a specific business. For example, you would expect the balance sheet of Sears to have a large accounts receivable balance.

■ **DIRECTIONS**

Examine the following list of accounts or financial statement characteristics and suggest an industry to which it may be related. There may be several acceptable industries for each characteristic, so be prepared to defend your answer.

Characteristic   **Industry**

1. A large investment in property, plant, & equipment relative
   to other assets   _____

2. Little or no accounts receivable   _____

3. A large amount of unearned revenue   _____

4. A significant amount of customer deposits   _____

5. A large warranty liability   _____

6. Inventory carried at fair market value   _____

7. A large obligation to a state agency   _____

8. An unusually large percentage of uncollectible accounts _____

No Pain, No Gain?

■ INTRODUCTION

As you know, revenue is ordinarily recognized at the point of sale (or exchange), when the earnings process is complete (or virtually complete) and when the amount of revenue can be objectively measured. For most businesses these tests are met when merchandise is sold or services are rendered. Like so many rules, the revenue recognition principle has exceptions in some unique cases, like long-term construction projects, certain farm products, or precious metals.

Consider the America Health Fitness Club that sells lifetime memberships for $1,000 each. Lifetime members are entitled to use of the facilities for the remainder of their lives. America's experience and research show that 70 percent of lifetime members stop attending and no longer use the facilities after one year. Another 20 percent use the facilities for approximately three years, and the remaining 10 percent continue to visit the health club throughout their lives.

■ DIRECTIONS

When do you believe a $1,000 receipt from a new lifetime member should be recognized as revenue?

Seaview Transportation Company

■ INTRODUCTION

The Seaview Transportation Company is a small, family-run business that has just completed its first year of operations. George Lazar, the general manager, has been eagerly awaiting the firm's financial statements to evaluate the outcome of the year's efforts. Marian Lazar, George's wife, is in charge of managing the office and generating all accounting information. Although Marian's background in accounting consists of two high school bookkeeping courses, George is unwilling to spend funds by hiring an accountant when Marian is so anxious to keep the books.

Throughout the year, she has continually claimed that the business was doing better than expected and that everything was looking fine. George, therefore, was disappointed and surprised to see the following income statement:

SEAVIEW TRANSPORTATION COMPANY
Income Statement
For the Year Ended December 31, 19X1

Revenues		
Fare revenue	$46,500	
Charter revenue	17,200	
Amounts due from customers	3,800	
Interest revenue	100	
Cash receipts from customers on account	13,400	
Increase in value of firm	5,000	
		$86,000
Expenses		
Vehicle leasing	$12,000	
Owner withdrawals	4,800	
Insurance	16,000	
Gas and oil	10,100	
Rent	1,800	
Supplies	400	
Wages	17,900	
Payroll taxes	3,500	
Advertising	500	
Payments on account	14,200	
Maintenance and repairs	1,500	
License expense	2,000	
Miscellaneous	1,100	
		85,800
Net income		$ 200

After a discussion, the couple decided to obtain your help in reviewing the company's records. They have asked you to determine whether profitability was calculated correctly. You have discovered the following items during the course of your examination:

1. Seaview opened a savings account at the American Savings Bank for $1,900 on January 3, 19X1. Interest earned totaled $100.
2. All charter trips were billed to customers on account.
3. During his first year of ownership, Lazar felt that he had made considerable progress toward improving customer service and satisfaction with Seaview Transportation. Many local residents agreed with him. Marian, therefore, increased the value of the firm by $5,000.
4. Cape Cod Auto Leasing provided vans for Seaview. A one-year contract was signed at the beginning of the year for $12,000, payable in three equal installments.
5. Insurance expense represents a two-year automobile policy that became effective on January 1, 19X1.
6. Maintenance and repairs are itemized as follows:

Van repairs	$1,200
Repairs to Lazar's personal car	300
	$1,500

A review of Seaview's cash receipts revealed that the firm was reimbursed $150 from Cape Cod Auto Leasing. This amount was for work Cape Cod should have performed prior to leasing the vans to Seaview. The reimbursement is not reflected in the preceding figures.

7. License expense includes $800 for a two-year city operating license granted on July 1, 19X1. In addition, a license fee of $700 pertaining to 19X1 and payable in 19X2 was incorrectly recorded as an addition to accounts payable and a deduction from fare revenue.

■ DIRECTIONS

Prepare a schedule or worksheet that demonstrates the adjustment of the income statement amounts to the appropriate balances. In class, you will need to be ready to discuss your schedule, which will be evaluated on its clarity and understandability. You should be prepared to explain each adjustment as if you were talking to Marian. Professionalism and courtesy are important.

The Closing

■ INTRODUCTION

Irwin Brenner recently retired and used $250,000 of his retirement benefits to open a restaurant. Brenner traveled extensively and did not want to be involved in the day-to-day operations. He selected Lee Kopek, an experienced restaurant manager, to oversee the business for him. As an incentive, Brenner gave Kopek a 50 percent share of any profits generated.

Kopek was delighted with the arrangement and worked hard to build a good customer base. Kopek asked Marty Raven, a waiter, to maintain the books and records for the restaurant. Raven had sat through three weeks of accounting principles at a local college, where he was a student.

At the end of the first year of operations, Raven presented the adjusted trial balance, which follows. The trial balance reflected Kopek's philosophy of renting all facilities and equipment and avoiding sales or purchases on credit.

Kopek understood that financial statements were needed, so she looked in the advertising section of the phone book and contacted Andrew Acarus to prepare the restaurant's financial statements from Raven's trial balance. Acarus prepared the statements and gave Kopek several schedules and a list of the necessary closing entries that she should record to begin the next accounting period. Kopek took the financial statements and stuffed Acarus' other schedules and papers under the seat of her car. She drove directly to Brenner's home.

Brenner quickly reviewed the income statement and was delighted with the results—a first-year profit of $250,000 (revenues of $400,000 less total expenses of $150,000). He thereupon authorized Kopek to withdraw $125,000 from the bank for her share of profits for the year. Kopek wrote herself a check for $125,000 and instructed Raven to make a journal entry for the payment by crediting cash and debiting intangible asset.

During the second year of operations, Kopek was content to rely on the stable customer base. At the end of the year, Raven prepared another adjusted trial balance, which also follows. Kopek looked in the telephone book again and chose Sarah Boyd to prepare the financial statements from Raven's trial balance. The scenario of the previous year occurred once again, with the space beneath Kopek's front seat continuing to serve as a filing cabinet for selected papers. Kopek received a $250,000 bonus, computed on the basis of a net income of $500,000. Raven recorded the bonus by increasing the intangible asset account by $250,000.

The scheme was replayed in years 3 and 4. Raven continued to prepare the adjusted trial balances (which also follow), and Kopek proceeded to engage a new accountant each year. Profits continued for the third and fourth years ($750,000 in year 3 and $1,000,000 in year 4). Brenner happily granted bonuses of $375,000 and $500,000, respectively.

Brenner's delight turned to confusion when he arrived at the restaurant one day for a meeting with Kopek and found a large sign on the door: CLOSED UNTIL FURTHER NOTICE. His confusion turned to panic when he discovered that the restaurant's bank account was empty.

ADJUSTED TRIAL BALANCES

	Year 1		Year 2		Year 3		Year 4	
Cash	$500,000		$ 625,000		$ 625,000		$ 500,000	
Intangible asset	—		125,000		375,000		750,000	
Irwin Brenner, capital		$250,000		$ 250,000		$ 250,000		$ 250,000
Revenue		400,000		800,000		1,200,000		1,600,000
Food & drink expense	100,000		200,000		300,000		400,000	
Utilities expense	10,000		18,000		30,000		36,000	
Rent expense	23,000		48,000		69,000		96,000	
Wages expenses	15,000		30,000		45,000		60,000	
Other expenses	2,000		4,000		6,000		8,000	
	$650,000	$650,000	$1,050,000	$1,050,000	$1,450,000	$1,450,000	$1,850,000	$1,850,000

■ DIRECTIONS

1. Briefly explain the purpose of closing entries.
2. Carefully evaluate the data presented in the trial balances. Does it appear that the books were ever closed? Explain the logic behind your response.
3. Compute the restaurant's correct income in each of the four years before considering any of the profit-sharing bonuses. Then briefly explain Kopek's scheme.
4. Why do you think that Kopek had Raven debit the bonuses to an asset account rather than an expense account?
5. What precautions can a silent (passive) investor like Brenner take to avoid this unfortunate predicament?

Kwik-Kleen, Inc.

■ INTRODUCTION

Kwik-Kleen is a medium-sized wholesaler of a broad line of industrial cleaning supplies. The company has experienced cash problems in recent months because its customers are not paying as promptly as they have in prior years. In fact, the average collection period has grown from 20 to 25 days, an increase of 25 percent.

Kwik-Kleen sells its products with terms of 1/10, n/30. In an attempt to improve collections, a new provision was added to the current credit terms to encourage more prompt payment by customers: an interest penalty of 1 percent per month would be applied to all account balances outstanding for more than 30 days. Kwik-Kleen management selected the 1 percent per month rate based on its recent experience with a local bank. The bank granted Kwik-Kleen a favorable 11 percent annual rate on a loan when most businesses were paying as much as 15 percent annually. Therefore, Kwik-Kleen's management figured that a 1 percent rate charged to customers is equivalent to 12 percent annually, one percentage point higher than the rate that the company has to pay on its loan.

After three months' experience with the revised credit terms, the average collection period has not improved. The two alternatives that follow were presented by the company's accounting department to achieve the original objective of reducing the length of time in which payments are received.

1. Increase the cash discount from 1 percent to 2 percent and maintain the 1 percent per month interest penalty.
2. Increase the interest penalty from 1 percent to 1.5 percent per month and maintain the cash discount.

Kwik-Kleen's management turned to its CPA for advice.

■ DIRECTIONS

1. Many businesses must obtain short-term loans in order to finance current operations and purchases of inventory. Explain to management why the 1 percent per month interest penalty did not reduce Kwik-Kleen's average collection period.
2. Discuss each of the two alternatives in terms of (a) their attractiveness to customers and (b) their attractiveness to Kwik-Kleen. Use a schedule with numbers if you believe it will make your presentation clearer.

The Great Escape

■ INTRODUCTION

Janine Hanckel owns and operates a sport fishing vessel called "The Great Escape." The boat caters to the tourist trade and can carry as many as 50 passengers. Occupancy has averaged 50 percent for the past several years. Due to bad weather conditions, the boat generally operates 280 days each year. The projected income statement for the upcoming accounting period is presented below.

The Great Escape
Projected Income Statement
For the Year Ended December 31, 19X4

Boarding fees ($35 per passenger)	$245,000
Operating expenses*	250,000
Net loss	$5,000

* Operating expenses include $3 per passenger for bait costs and $2 per passenger for city harbor fees.

Hanckel uses a cash-only policy in running the business. No personal checks or credit are accepted, and no credit-card sales are made. Hanckel has noticed that some of her competitors have begun to accept other forms of payment, and those skippers have had higher occupancy rates lately. Hanckel is disturbed, because "The Great Escape" consistently "out-fishes" the other boats.

Hanckel has discussed the problem with her CPA. The CPA told her that sales normally increase when customers are permitted to use personal checks or bank credit cards, but that most cash customers also change payment methods when alternatives are available. At the end of their meeting Hanckel's CPA estimated that:

1. 90 percent of the customers would use a bank credit card, on which a 5 percent service charge would be imposed by the bank.
2. 5 percent of the customers would pay by check.
3. Approximately 20 percent of the checks written would never clear because of nonsufficient funds (NSF).
4. 5 percent of the customers would continue to pay with cash.
5. The boat occupancy rate would increase from 50 percent to 60 percent.
6. Operating expenses (exclusive of bait costs and harbor fees) would rise by 3 percent as a result of the increased passenger load.

■ DIRECTIONS

1. Prepare an analysis showing the attractiveness of the alternative methods of payment (i.e., cash-only versus cash, checks, and credit cards).
2. Based on your schedule, determine whether you would advise Hanckel to change her payment policy.
3. What other factors should be considered in the decision to change from a cash-only policy?

In One Door and Out the Other

■ INTRODUCTION

The Body Hanger, a clothing store that specializes in high-fashion merchandise, is located at a regional shopping mall. Sales over the past few years have averaged approximately $120,000 per month. Merchandise is priced consistently at 250 percent of cost.

Lynn Land was recently hired as a special marketing consultant in an effort to boost sales. Land immediately recommended that the single door, which was tended by a fancily attired doorman, be replaced with an "open wall" concept. The new concept would save the cost of the doorman and allow patrons to enter and exit along the entire front of the store.

The following data relate to the three-month period following the implementation of the "open wall" design.

	Month 1	Month 2	Month 3
Purchases (at cost)	$ 70,000	$ 91,000	$ 65,000
Purchases returns (at cost)	3,000	—	5,000
Sales	160,000	210,000	190,000
Sales returns	5,000	10,000	25,000

The cost of inventory on hand at the beginning of the first month was $150,000. A physical inventory count at the end of the third month revealed an actual ending inventory cost of $90,000.

■ DIRECTIONS

Comment on the success or failure of the "open wall" concept.

Depreciation Tune-up

■ INTRODUCTION

Tom Ferguson and Cindy Zamora were friends at Midwestern University several years ago. Cindy graduated and started working at First Trust Bank, where she is now a loan officer. Tom left school and started an auto repair shop with $185,000 that had been willed to him by a wealthy relative.

Tom purchased all the equipment he needed for $150,000 cash. He kept the remaining cash to cover his operating costs. Tom depreciated the equipment over 15 years using the sum-of-the-years'-digits method and assuming no salvage value.

The equipment is now fully depreciated and must be replaced. Tom will not be able to sell any of the equipment, so he has decided to throw it all away at the local dump once he gets his new equipment. After shopping around, he has discovered that the replacement cost of the equipment is four times the amount he originally paid for it.

Tom has been fortunate enough to achieve profits in every year of operation. However, each year Tom withdrew cash in an amount equal to the net income reported on the income statement.

Tom gathers all of his financial statements for the last 15 years and makes an appointment with Cindy to discuss a loan to finance the new equipment.

■ DIRECTIONS

1. How much cash does Tom have in his business account when he goes to see Cindy? Assume that there were no significant changes in inventories, receivables, and payables. Disregard income taxes.

2. In light of Tom's experience with the high costs of replacing the equipment, can the manner in which he determined depreciation expense (i.e., based on its historical cost) be criticized? Explain you answer and comment on the impact of his withdrawal policy.

Henderson and Associates

■ INTRODUCTION

Henderson and Associates is a corporation engaged in the development and production of television programs for commercial sponsorship. The costs of each program are accounted for separately as intangible assets and are carried on Henderson's books as follows:

Program	Development Costs*
"I Live Alone"	$900,000
"Jack Gannon, M.D."	640,000
"512 Oak Lane"	310,000
"Hollywood"	180,000

* Prior to recording amortization for the current year.

An examination of contracts and records revealed the following information at year-end:

1. The first two accounts listed represent the total cost of completed programs that were televised during the accounting period just ended. Under the terms of an existing contract, "I Live Alone" will be rerun during the next accounting period at a fee equal to 50 percent of the fee for the first run. The contract for the first broadcast run produced $80,000 of revenue. The sponsor's contract for "Jack Gannon, M.D." stipulates that the program can be rerun during the next season at a fee equal to 75 percent of the fee on the first run. No present indications exist that the program will be rerun.

2. The balance in the "512 Oak Lane" account is the cost of a new program that has just been completed and is being considered by several companies for commercial sponsorship.

3. The balance in the "Hollywood" account represents the cost of a partially completed program for a projected series that has been abandoned.

■ DIRECTIONS

1. Briefly describe the general principles of accounting on which amortization is based.

2. How would you report the balances of these accounts in Henderson's financial statements? Explain your answer by making specific references to the balance sheet and income statement presentations.

Pop Pop

■ INTRODUCTION

On Wednesday, October 21, 1992, the pop singing group, New Kids on the Block, filed a lawsuit against Button Master of Bridgeport, Pennsylvania. The pop group went to court in an effort to force the company to stop making buttons using their pictures. According to their attorney, the lawsuit seeks more than $75,000 for violations of the trademark law.

On the same day in Atlanta, Elton John filed a suit against the tabloid show "Hard Copy," accusing extortion, slander, invasion of privacy, and reckless endangerment. The British pop star is seeking at least $35 million in damages against the show's producers for alleged comments and speculative remarks made by a reporter off the air.

■ DIRECTIONS

1. Assume that you were the accountant consulted by the New Kids on the Block. Describe some of the factors you considered in deciding that the damages were approximately $75,000.
2. Elton John's suit seeks considerably more in damages. Without discussing the merits or issues of the case, what financial aspects may have contributed to his request for such a high amount?

Exchanging Your Way to Profitability?

■ INTRODUCTION

Alamo Manufacturing and Griffin Motors both manufacture specialized sports cars for a limited market. Each company has experienced an excessive buildup of inventory in recent months because of a sluggish market for their cars.

The cars manufactured by each company have different styling features but are similar in cost and market values. Each item of inventory has an average cost of about $25,000 and an average sales price of $40,000.

The owners of each company met over lunch one day and discussed the economy and their respective problems. In the course of their meal they came up with a great idea to help each other—they agreed to exchange 100 cars from their inventories in a cash-free transaction. In other words, Alamo will "sell" 100 cars to Griffin for $4,000,000 and Griffin will "sell" 100 cars to Alamo for the same amount. The companies plan to record a $15,000 gain per unit as a result of this exchange. Profitability will be increased, as will inventory asset values. The owners are pleased with their creative solution to their common plight.

■ DIRECTIONS

Comment on the likely success or failure of this plan from an accounting point of view.

Foreign Operations

■ **INTRODUCTION**

Globalization is a term used often in discussing business these days. Foreign operations are now a key factor in the business plans of most major U.S.-based corporations. Growth of foreign trade and multinational corporations have also brought increased attention to the accounting consequences.

Assume that you are the controller for a medium-sized company that is considering its first overseas expansion in Russia. You have been asked to participate in a strategy session concerning the proposed new operation.

■ **DIRECTIONS**

1. What are some reasons that your company should consider establishing an operation beyond its own national borders?
2. What are some potential problems that should be anticipated?
3. Specifically, what accounting consequences can be expected if the new venture occurs?

Partner Squeeze Play

■ INTRODUCTION

Leland McKenzie is the senior partner of the L.A. law firm McKenzie, Brackman. His father founded the firm with Douglas Brackman's father many years ago. For nearly 40 years Leland himself has been effectively building the practice and has been a distinguished member of the legal community.

In recent years he has become disgusted with the activities and operations of the firm. He is not pleased with the quality of the associates the firm has hired. He is dissatisfied with the business activities of some clients that have retained the firm. He is at odds with most of the partners. In short, he is ready to retire.

The partnership agreement stipulates that a retiring partner may negotiate the amount of withdrawal for settlement purposes. McKenzie's capital balance is presently $350,000. His profit sharing ratio is 30 percent, and his earnings have averaged $220,000 over the last five years. Recently, he has been more active in the management of the firm than in client work. Gross revenues of the firm have averaged $7 million during the last few years.

■ DIRECTIONS

1. Assume that you are Leland McKenzie. What do you think would be a fair amount to receive at your withdrawal? Explain the issues that contributed to your suggestion.
2. Assume that you are Douglas Brackman, the next most senior partner. What types of issues would you present at a partners' meeting to discuss the settlement of McKenzie's retirement?
3. Assume that you are one of the other partners. What points would you make in the negotiations?

The Value of Reporting

■ INTRODUCTION

Julia Arana is the president of Arana Real Estate Development Company. She has generated a successful business in the last few years by acquiring real estate from bankruptcy proceedings or other court-ordered liquidations. The company makes needed improvements to the properties and resells them for sizable profits. Arana has high expectations for the future of her company.

She understands that the accounting information used in her financial reports should be relevant and reliable. After much consideration, she has decided that the historical cost method presently used by the company does not provide information that is relevant. She believes that current value information would be more meaningful to users of the company's financial statements in view of the nature of her business.

Arana has come to you, her accountant, for advice in the revision of her financial statements so that they reflect the current value of her business.

■ DIRECTIONS

1. Explain the meaning of the terms *relevant* and *reliable* as used in the preparation of financial statements.
2. Review the concepts of historical cost and current value in the context of reporting requirements.
3. Suggest some reporting options that may help ease Arana's concern and allow the company to report the type of information that she wants.

Quicksand Advice

■ INTRODUCTION

Joseph Skaggs owned 100 shares of common stock of Richland Corporation. Skaggs had acquired the stock at $50 per share and was disappointed to see its value rapidly drop to $40 per share. Skaggs asked his friend, Glenda Worsham, to give her opinion about the Richland stock performance. Worsham quickly reviewed Richland's balance sheet and calculated the book value to be about $38 per share of common stock. Worsham told Skaggs not to be too concerned because the stock should be worth at least its book value per share, and was probably worth more because assets are often understated on the balance sheet.

Skaggs took comfort in the advice and continued to hold the stock while its value slipped to $30 per share, then to $20 per share, and finally to $7 per share. Skaggs contacted Worsham again to ask how her evaluation could be so wrong. Upon closer examination of Richland's balance sheet, Worsham noticed a significant amount of goodwill listed as an asset. A note to the financial statements explained that several years ago Richland had acquired a number of subsidiaries at prices in excess of their underlying asset values. Lately the acquired companies have not been performing as well as they had when acquired.

■ DIRECTIONS

1. Briefly explain how Worsham calculated Richland's book value per common share.
2. Define goodwill from an accounting perspective. Comment on the reasons that a company would purchase a company for a price that exceeds the current value of the assets and liabilities acquired.
3. Describe the critical error of Worsham's original evaluation of Richland's stock.

Treasured Treasury Stock

■ INTRODUCTION

Amalgamated Enterprises is a corporation that has shares widely held by a number of investors. The shares of stock are currently trading at $40 per share. Jim Rice owns approximately 10 percent of the outstanding shares. Rice is very displeased with Amalgamated's current management and has repeatedly demanded performance improvements. Recently, Rice wrote to Amalgamated's other shareholders and asked them to join him in a vote to fire the current management team.

To rid themselves of the pesky stockholder, the company's management offered Rice $50 per share for all of the stock that he holds. Rice is likely to accept the offer.

The company will have to pay $3 million in excess of current market value for Rice's shares. Amalgamated's management proposes to account for the purchase of Rice's stock as a treasury stock transaction.

■ DIRECTIONS

1. What are the basic rules of accounting for treasury stock transactions?
2. Will Amalgamated record the $3 million as a loss on the company's books?
3. If you were one of Amalgamated's other stockholders, how would you regard the company's offer to Rice?

Bonded

■ **INTRODUCTION**

Several years ago Keaton Corporation issued $10 million of 10 percent bonds. The bonds are callable at 105 at any time prior to maturity. In addition, each $1,000 bond is convertible into 40 shares of Keaton's common stock. The conversion privilege can be exercised at the option of the bondholder. In the event that Keaton decides to call the bonds, the bondholders may either elect to exercise the conversion feature or accept the call price. Keaton has never paid a dividend on its common stock.

■ **DIRECTIONS**

Assume that you are a holder of some of Keaton's bonds. Answer the following questions.

1. What is the minimum price per share that the common stock would have to reach before you would consider converting your bonds?

2. If Keaton's stock was trading at $50 per share when the bonds had five years until maturity, would you want to exercise your conversion privilege? Briefly explain your reasoning.

Puff the Magic Company

■ INTRODUCTION

Linda Glisson recently formed three separate companies. These companies had the respective duties of acquiring materials, repackaging the materials, and distributing the materials. Each company was formed with a $10,000 initial capital investment. The acquisition company acquired $10,000 of merchandise using the cash Glisson had invested. The acquisition company in turn resold the merchandise to the packaging company for $20,000, on account. The packaging company sold the same merchandise to the distribution company for $40,000 on account.

Glisson's accountant prepared financial statements for each of the three separate companies. The acquisition company's balance sheet revealed receivables of $20,000 and equity of $20,000. The packaging company's balance sheet showed cash of $10,000, receivables of $40,000, payables of $20,000, and equity of $30,000. Finally, the distribution company's balance sheet disclosed cash of $10,000, inventory of $40,000, payables of $40,000, and equity of $10,000.

■ DIRECTIONS

1. Verify the amounts presented on the three separate balance sheets.
2. Assume that you are a bank officer who is considering a loan to Glisson and her companies. Describe your unwillingness to rely on three separate balance sheets as the basis for your decision.
3. Given the facts, what do you think the proper balance sheet amounts should be? Try to deduce the amounts by preparing formal worksheets.

Ryan's Hope

■ INTRODUCTION

Ryan Corporation operates a wholesale food business. The company has grown quickly in its six years of existence, necessitating substantial bank borrowing to support the higher level of sales, receivables, and merchandise inventory. The president of Ryan, Chip Hilton, wants to increase the present bank loans from $60,000 to $75,000 to provide more working capital. Ryan's accountant, on the other hand, believes that Ryan should generate more cash by using internal policies. The accountant explained to Hilton, "There's no interest charged on the money that you are able to generate internally by more efficient operations."

The accountant has offered some policy changes for Hilton to consider. The recommendations are based on the fact that Ryan's average daily credit sales amount to $4,400 at a gross profit rate of 15 percent (using a 360-day year), average receivables for the year are $88,000 and average inventories are $134,640.

After a meeting to discuss alternatives, Hilton and the management team have narrowed the alternatives down to the following two:

1. Increase accounts receivable turnover by two, by sending out invoices sooner and calling on delinquent accounts.
2. Increase inventory turnover by one, by more selective ordering of slow-moving merchandise.

■ DIRECTIONS

1. If both policy changes are implemented, how much additional cash could be obtained to support Ryan's growth? Defend your position with a schedule.
2. What other alternatives are available to Ryan to accelerate cash inflows from receivables and inventory?

Grocery Operations:
Slash and Burn or Rise and Shine?

■ INTRODUCTION

Slice Food Stores is a modest retail grocery chain that has been in existence for many years as a relatively profitable operation. Slice advertises itself as a low-cost, no-frills operation, and sells a variety of products other than typical groceries. Examples include health and beauty aids, flowers, bakery goods, film processing services, automotive maintenance items, pet supplies, plastic products, children's toys, school supplies, and drugs (in a pharmacy).

Slice recently hired a hard-nosed operations manager who is determined to raise the chain's profitability. He instituted two new strategies for Slice. First, he decided to eliminate all products that he believed did not absorb the overhead allocated to them. He required the accounting department to prepare a full cost analysis of every product sold. His directions were very specific that all operating expenses and other overhead should be allocated to products based on square footage of floor space consumed by the products. After reviewing the analysis prepared by the accountant, he noticed many products that sold in excess of their variable costs, but were unable to absorb the overhead that had been allocated to them. The manager suspended sales of those products, and continued this policy for several more months.

The manager's second aggressive strategy was to implement a "zone pricing" plan, whereby prices were imposed at higher levels in less competitive markets like small towns, while prices for the same products were lower in more competitive metropolitan areas. Part of this pricing strategy was to adopt absurdly low prices when entering a new market. Although large losses would initially occur for a new store, his plan was to drive competition out of the market and then to raise prices back to higher levels. The manager concluded that this strategy could be sustained because Slice has numerous profitable operations that could cushion the losses on new markets without a significant adverse effect on overall corporate profitability.

■ DIRECTIONS

1. Describe the problems in the manager's strategy to eliminate products whose profits were insufficient to cover the overhead allocation.
2. Assess the potential for success or failure of the zone pricing strategy. Include a consideration of the ethics of such business strategies.

The Heart of Profitability

■ INTRODUCTION

Quest Medical Equipment Corporation manufactures a unique heart monitor device that is sold primarily to hospitals and medical schools. The product is patented, sells for approximately $1,000 per unit, and costs $1,500 per unit to manufacture. Use of the heart monitor requires the consumption of a special package of Quest electronic stick-on tabs. A package of the tabs costs $.10 to manufacture, but sells for $2.00. Estimates are that each heart monitor sold will result in first-year sales of 100 packages of the stick-on tabs and annual sales of 500 packages after the first year.

Obviously, Quest is interested in selling the heart monitor, even at a loss, in order to tap into a captive market for future sales of stick-on tabs. Each heart monitor has an estimated useful life of approximately 10 years.

■ DIRECTIONS

1. Prepare a financial analysis that demonstrates the overall profitability associated with the sale of a single heart monitor. Indicate which year will show enough profit to cover the initial losses associated with a single monitor.
2. Quest plans to sell 7,000 monitors during the first year of operations and realizes that a substantial accounting loss will result. Discuss how Quest's management might effectively communicate its financial prospects while still complying with generally accepted accounting principles.

Springfield Corporation's Budgeting Process

■ INTRODUCTION

Springfield Corporation is a manufacturing company with a calendar year-end. The company starts to formulate its annual budget in the August before the budget year begins. Budgeting begins with the president, who is the chief operating officer of the corporation. The president establishes target amounts for the total dollar sales and net income before taxes.

The sales target is given to the marketing department, where the marketing manager formulates a sales budget by product line in both units and dollars. Each of the corporation's five sales districts are given sales quotas in dollars and units for each product line sold in their district. The marketing manager also estimates the cost of the marketing activities required to support the target sales volume and prepares a tentative marketing expense budget.

The executive vice-president then uses the information assembled (the sales and profit targets, the sales budget by product line, and the tentative marketing expense budget) to determine the dollar amounts that can be devoted to manufacturing and corporate office expense. The executive vice-president prepares the budget for all the corporate expenses and then forwards the product line sales budget (in units and dollars) to the production department.

The production manager is responsible for the manufacturing plan that will produce the required units, on time, within the cost constraints set by the executive vice-president. The production manager calls a meeting of the factory managers, and the budgeting process usually comes to a halt at this point. The factory managers and the production manager invariably consider the financial resources allocated to them to be inadequate.

When such a standstill occurs, the vice-president of finance, the executive vice-president, the marketing manager, and the production manager meet to determine the final budgets for each of the areas. This meeting is usually heated and generally results in a modest increase in the total amount available for manufacturing costs, while marketing and corporate expense budgets are cut. The total sales and net income figures proposed by the president are seldom changed.

Although the participants are rarely pleased with the compromises, these budgets are final. Each executive then develops a new detailed budget for the operations in his or her area.

None of the areas has achieved its budget in recent years. Sales often run below the target. When budgeted sales are not achieved, each area is expected to cut costs so that the president's profit target can still be met. Despite the cost cutting, the profit target is seldom met because costs cannot be cut enough. In fact, costs lately have run above the original budget in all functional areas.

The president, disturbed that Springfield has not been able to meet the sales and profit targets, recently hired a consultant with considerable experience in the industry. The consultant reviewed the budgets for the past four years and believed that the product line sales budgets were reasonable and that the cost and expense budgets were adequate for the budgeted sales and production levels.

■ DIRECTIONS

1. Discuss how the budgeting process used by Springfield Corporation contributes to the failure to achieve the president's sales and profit targets.
2. Suggest how Springfield's budgeting process could be revised to correct the problems.

Flying Too High?

■ INTRODUCTION

Fly High, Inc., produces a line of kites that are very popular with children. The manufacturing process consists of three phases: printing, cutting, and packaging. Large sheets of lightweight plastic are first printed with cartoon characters and then cut. In another department, plastic rods are cut and notched to form the crosspieces for the kites. Finally, the sheets and crosspieces are packaged in a clear plastic container.

Bill Strong, the production manager, has been beset with complaints from upper management about declining gross profit. Strong wrote a memo that stated, "Costs are going up, and I can't help that." Front office investigation revealed that prices paid for direct material and labor do not account for much of the decline in gross profit. Strong has challenged management to prove that the gross profit decline has been the result of production inefficiency.

You are the assistant to the controller and have been asked to participate in the investigation. The following information has been collected for your use:

1. The printing operation should take 5 minutes per dozen kites, including set-up and inspection.
2. The sheet-cutting operation should take 10 minutes per dozen kites, including set-up and inspection.
3. The rod-cutting operation should take 10 minutes per dozen kites, including set-up and inspection.
4. The packaging operation should take 5 minutes per dozen kites.
5. Printing, cutting, and packaging employees are normally paid $6.00 per hour.
6. Each plastic sheet generally costs $3.60 and can be cut into one dozen kites.
7. Six 12-foot plastic rods usually cost $6.00 and can be cut into 24 crosspieces, adequate for one dozen kites.
8. The clear plastic packing material costs $1.20 per dozen kites.

At the end of the month, you determined that 12,000 kites have been produced. Direct labor payroll amounted to $3,900 for the 600 hours worked. Eleven hundred plastic sheets were purchased at $4.00 each, and all were used. In addition, 8,000 plastic rods were purchased for $8,500, but only 6,800 rods were used.

■ DIRECTIONS

In your role as assistant controller, prepare an analysis of the standard costs and variances, and explain the likely causes of the variances you derive. Identify those variances for which Strong could be held responsible. If Strong is not responsible, suggest who is.

A Safe System?

■ INTRODUCTION

Granite, Inc. is a manufacturer of high-quality safes for home and office use. The safes are carefully crafted from the best steel available and equipped with patented locking devices that reflect the latest technology.

The president of Granite owns and operates several other businesses. Although he visits the factory on an irregular basis, he insists on strict quality control, complete customer satisfaction, and profitable performance.

Granite recently accepted a "rush order" from a large gun store. Additional steel had to be ordered and was received in a special overnight shipment. The steel was not hardened to Granite's normal specifications, but manufacturing personnel decided to use it anyway because of the time constraints. The purchasing department was notified of the inferior quality and was able to negotiate a 40 percent reduction in the invoice price of the material. Since the steel was not as hard as it should have been, shop employees were able to cut, weld, drill, and bend the steel in about half of the normal time.

■ DIRECTIONS

1. Discuss how a responsibility accounting system might be used and why it would be helpful to Granite's owner.
2. Assume the role of Granite's production supervisor. Describe the probable impact of the gun store order on the variances for which you are held accountable.
3. Assume the role of Granite's purchasing department manager. Describe the probable impact of the gun store order on the variances for which you are held accountable.
4. After considering these positions, what can you recommend to help Granite ensure a "safe" responsibility accounting system?

Viceroy Corporation

■ INTRODUCTION

The Viceroy Corporation is a small manufacturer of workshop tools. The company generates an adequate profit by operating a single eight-hour shift at its plant. Presently, the plant produces 380,000 units of finished products per year. Although various goods are involved, production personnel estimate that the average direct labor time to complete one unit is 15 minutes. Viceroy currently utilizes 95 percent of its operating capacity.

Management is contemplating a change in operations. Part A402 is now purchased from outside suppliers at a cost of $4.25 per unit. Recently, Viceroy has had significant problems with the supplier's reliability, so the company is studying the feasibility of producing the part itself. The following information pertinent to the production of part A402 has been gathered:

> Annual volume needed: 36,000 units
> Estimated direct material cost per unit: $1.45
> Estimated direct labor cost per unit: $1.00 (10 minutes at $6.00 per hour)
> Estimated variable factory overhead per unit: $0.75
> Estimated fixed factory overhead:
>> Annual rental of a special machine: $12,500
>> Annual salary of new production supervisor: $18,000

Part A402 will also require some machine time on existing equipment, and the related costs are included in the above estimates. The special machine that will be rented will not be used for any other purposes, and so will not affect Viceroy's other productive capacity.

■ DIRECTIONS

Assume that you are the plant manger for Viceroy. What questions would you want answered before authorizing the in-house production of part A402, and what specific financial data would you gather as part of the decision-making process?

Is This Ivory Pure?

■ INTRODUCTION

Ivory Company has just concluded its worst year since beginning operations five years ago. The firm's income statement is as follows:

Ivory Company
Income Statement
For the Year Ended December 31, 19X3

Sales (15,000 units @ $10)		$ 150,000
Cost of goods sold:		
Beginning inventory (5,000 units @ $6)	$ 30,000	
Cost of goods manufactured (15,000 @ $6)	90,000	
Goods available for sale	$120,000	
Less ending inventory (5,000 @ $6)	30,000	
Cost of goods sold		90,000
Gross profit		$ 60,000
Selling and administrative expenses		70,000
Net loss		$ (10,000)

In the preparation of this income statement, the accountant noted that cost of goods manufactured contained $30,000 of fixed overhead; the remaining production costs were variable and amounted to $4 per unit.

The company's board of directors fired the president and searched for a successor. An applicant agreed to take the job for a bonus of 50 percent of any increase in gross profit generated and also agreed to reimburse the company for any losses incurred. The board hired the applicant without further discussion.

Soon after the new president took over, Ivory was running at full capacity. The income statement for the next period showed an increase in gross profit even though there had been no growth in sales volume or sales pricing. The cost behavior patterns were identical to those of the previous year (presented above). The president accepted the bonus and abruptly resigned, leaving the board of directors baffled.

■ DIRECTIONS

What do you think the new president did to increase gross profit when neither the sales nor the cost patterns had changed? Determine the impact on ending inventory, cost of goods sold, and net income. (Hint: no numerical calculations are required to answer these questions.)

Bulldog Enterprises

▪ INTRODUCTION

Bulldog Enterprises is a small manufacturer of textile machinery. Management has received several project proposals to consider when formulating next year's capital budget. Bulldog's management requires a 14 percent return on its investment. The following is a list of the proposals with all relevant increases to revenue or cost savings included:

Project	Initial Investment	Net Annual Cash Inflows	Project Life	Present Value of Net Annual Cash Inflows	Net Present Value
A	$14,000	$4,000	5	$13,732	
B	15,000	6,000	4	17,482	
C	10,000	3,000	8	13,917	
D	15,000	4,000	6	15,555	
E	15,000	3,500	10	18,256	
F	10,000	2,332	7	10,000	
G	18,000	6,000	5	20,598	
H	50,000	15,000	4	43,706	
I	20,000	3,500	6	13,610	
J	25,000	5,054	9	25,000	

The major limiting factor is the availability of funding for the proposed projects. Management believes that it can afford to invest $55,000, with an increase of 10 percent if necessary. Bulldog uses the net present value to evaluate its prospective capital investments.

▪ DIRECTIONS

Assume that you are part of the team assigned with the task of making the final selection of projects. Recommend those projects that Bulldog should undertake.

PART 2

Critical Reading
and
Research Assignments

Origins of Accounting Terminology

■ INTRODUCTION

Have you ever been curious about the origins of some accounting terms? Many are derivatives of Latin words, although some evolved from other languages. Knowing the origins of words (called *etymology*) may help you understand their current context.

■ DIRECTIONS

For each of the following accounting terms, find the language of origin and what the word first meant. (Hint: Almost any dictionary will be a good source, but the November 1984 issue of *Practical Accountant* has a thorough and interesting page that will also help.)

Word	Original Language and Word	Original Meaning
1. Debit	_____	_____
2. Credit	_____	_____
3. Asset	_____	_____
4. Liability	_____	_____
5. Capital	_____	_____
6. Journal	_____	_____
7. Account	_____	_____
8. Depreciate	_____	_____
9. Amortize	_____	_____
10. Corporation	_____	_____
11. Budget	_____	_____
12. Loss	_____	_____
13. Earnings	_____	_____
14. Revenue	_____	_____
15. Taxation	_____	_____

Functions, Functions, Everywhere a Function

■ **INTRODUCTION**

Most electronic spreadsheets have a number of built-in functions embedded in their underlying program structure. For example, many programs can calculate and provide details regarding the depreciation of an asset's cost using alternative methods presented in accounting principles. Learning the existence and accessibility of such functions can make the computations required in accounting much easier.

■ **DIRECTIONS**

This assignment requires a close inspection of an electronic spreadsheet software package of your choice. Obtain a copy of the user's manual (or other documentation) and identify the imbedded program commands or functions that would be useful in various accounting applications. Use the form on the next page to list as many functions as possible.

Spreadsheet program   _____

Name of manual reviewed   _____

Function	Keystroke Command	Accounting Application
_____	_____	_____
_____	_____	_____
_____	_____	_____
_____	_____	_____
_____	_____	_____
_____	_____	_____
_____	_____	_____
_____	_____	_____
_____	_____	_____
_____	_____	_____
_____	_____	_____
_____	_____	_____
_____	_____	_____
_____	_____	_____
_____	_____	_____
_____	_____	_____
_____	_____	_____
_____	_____	_____
_____	_____	_____
_____	_____	_____

Summary of Significant Accounting Policies

■ **INTRODUCTION**

The first note to the financial statements of almost every company is entitled "Summary of Significant Accounting Policies." This note is required, and summarizes in one location the basic accounting policies used by the reporting company. This note is critical because it reveals the accounting methods selected by a company. The methods selected may affect a user's interpretation of the financial statements.

■ **DIRECTIONS**

You should locate a financial statement for a company of your choice. Make a copy of the first note included in the financial statement and bring it to class for discussion.

Translating Accounting

■ INTRODUCTION

Many financial accounting standards and rules describe the procedures and processes to be followed when accounting for specific transactions and events. Properly trained accountants (and other business people) need to be able to read the technical words in a standard, understand the meaning, and then apply the prescription to a particular situation.

The following assignments involve locating an accounting standard written by the Financial Accounting Standards Board. You will read the standard (abbreviated SFAS) and determine the answers to the questions listed below. Although many of the topics are too rigorous for a thorough presentation in your principles course, you should have no difficulty finding the answers to the specific questions.

■ DIRECTIONS

Follow your instructor's request to investigate the appropriate accounting treatment of one of the following topics. Find the standard listed and answer the questions.

1. SFAS No. 2 concerns research and development costs.

    How are all research and development costs of all enterprises accounted for? Name five activities considered to be research and development according to the standard. If your company invests heavily in research, would you favor or dislike this accounting treatment? Why?

2. SFAS No. 7 prescribes the appropriate accounting treatment for developmental stage enterprises.

    How is a developmental stage enterprise defined? SFAS No. 7 allows a special accounting treatment for such enterprises; what is the treatment allowed? Does the special treatment pertain exclusively to supplemental disclosures or does it change the basic content of financial statements?

3. SFAS No. 13 governs accounting for leases.

    What is the definition of a *capital lease*? What is the definition of *minimum lease payment*? What are the four major criteria that are used in deciding whether a lease is a capital lease? If you are the controller for a company that is interested in minimizing income taxes, which type of lease might you try to negotiate, and why?

4. SFAS No. 14 sets the standards for financial reporting for segments of a business.

   What are the three major tests associated with the process of identifying a significant industry segment? What is the suggested maximum number of segments that should be reported? Where in the financial statements will you find segment information? Which companies must adhere to the reporting requirements of SFAS No. 14?

5. SFAS No. 34 describes a process whereby interest is capitalized on self-constructed assets.

   What are the general rules for the determination of a qualifying asset? What are the three conditions that must be met before the capitalization period can begin? What is meant by the term *avoidable interest*? Briefly describe the purpose for this standard.

6. SFAS No. 43 relates to compensated absences.

   How is a period of compensated absence defined? What are several items that are specifically excluded from the provisions of this statement? What are some of the criteria that should be applied in deciding whether costs should be accrued for periods of compensated absences? What is an example of a journal entry (no numbers) that might be necessary at the end of an accounting period because of this accounting rule?

7. SFAS No. 52 is called "Foreign Currency Translation."

   Probably the most important term in the statement is *functional currency*. How is it defined, and what are six factors used in its determination? What are the two categories into which SFAS No. 52 divides foreign currency accounting? What is the definition given for *current exchange rate*?

8. SFAS No. 87 prescribes the accounting treatment of employers' accounting for pensions.

   What is a defined benefit pension plan? Contrast a defined benefit plan with a defined contribution plan. As an employee, which would you prefer based on the definitions in the standard? Paraphrase the definitions of a projected benefit obligation and an accumulated benefit obligation. Which will always be larger?

9. SFAS No. 89 is entitled "Financial Reporting and Changing Prices."

   How many FASB publications are superseded by SFAS No. 89? What does this standard recommend? Based on your review of SFAS No. 89, do you think that there will be any more statements concerning this topic? Why or why not?

10. After years of controversy concerning the proper accounting for income taxes, the FASB issued SFAS No. 109.

    Briefly describe what is meant by a *temporary difference,* and then give an example of it. Can the approach advocated by SFAS No. 109 be considered a balance sheet or an income statement emphasis? Assuming that a deferred tax liability exists for a company, give the journal entry (no numbers) that would be made at year-end.

High-Tech Crime

■ INTRODUCTION

In an article that focused on computer fraud, *The Wall Street Journal* reported the following:

> At its London office, American Telephone & Telegraph Co. says, three technicians used a computer to funnel company funds into their own pockets. At General Dynamics Corp.'s space division in San Diego, an employee plotted to sabotage the company by wiping out a computer program used to build missiles. And at Charles Schwab & Co. headquarters in San Francisco, some employees used the stock brokerage firm's computer system to buy and sell cocaine.
>
> As these examples suggest, employees are finding increasingly ingenious ways to misuse their companies' computer systems. Although publicity about computer wrongdoing has often focused on outside hackers gaining entry to systems to wreak havoc, insiders are proving far more adept at creating computer havoc. Workers may use company computer systems to line their own pockets, to seek revenge because they didn't get a promotion or because of other perceived slights....[1]

Computer fraud is not new—it has been around almost as long as computers have. It is becoming more troublesome, though, as workers gain added computer expertise. Combine this expertise with more powerful desktops and laptops (units that can easily tap into huge corporate data bases) and a genuine control problem is created.

■ DIRECTIONS

1. Form a team with one other member of your class. Write a one-paragraph description of at least three creative schemes that have involved an employee's use of a computer to defraud a company or governmental unit. The necessary information may be obtained from library research or by talking with knowledgeable professionals.

2. For each scheme described, write a second paragraph that suggests computer or procedural controls that may have prevented or detected such schemes.

---

[1] "Rigging Computers for Fraud or Malice Is Often an Inside Job," *The Wall Street Journal* (August 27, 1992), pp. A1, A4.

I Want to Buy a Sports Team

■ INTRODUCTION

Your client, Michael McLeod, has had a successful career in publishing over the last 20 years. Through a series of business acquisitions and timely investments, McLeod and his family have accumulated a net worth of approximately $250 million.

You have been asked to gather some preliminary information in response to the family's interest in the acquisition of a major league sports franchise, and you recall reading an article that may serve as a helpful starting point: "Big Leagues, Bad Business," *Financial World* (July 7, 1992), pp. 34-35, 38-39, 42-51.

■ DIRECTIONS

1. Obtain a copy of the *Financial World* article from your library. Using the facts in the article, list the five most valuable major league sports franchises and the five most profitable. Explain the difference between the valuation of a franchise and the profitability. Include a brief evaluation of the factors that authors used to determine "value" and "profitability."

2. Write a one-page recommendation to McLeod outlining your conclusions and reasons for buying (or not buying) a major league sports franchise at this time.

The Windbag Theory

■ INTRODUCTION

Company recruiters characterize today's business graduates as masters of the technical skills related to their chosen areas of study. However, businesses give low marks to these same graduates when they are asked to write a report to a potential client, a letter to a supplier, or even an inner-office memo. If business communication skills are deteriorating, students in a highly technical discipline such as accounting must take special care to improve their writing abilities. Accounting is full of complex rules and has a unique jargon. A genuine problem exists for graduates who must use accounting information to make decisions but cannot write clearly.

Presentation skills perhaps vary with the type of information that one is trying to communicate. Consider the so-called "windbag theory" advanced by two reporters from *Forbes* magazine. The reporters noted that:

> A strange thing seems to happen to companies when their businesses begin to deteriorate. The chairman's letter to shareholders in the annual report often becomes windier than ever. Paragraphs grow gassy and obese; dependent clauses pile up; thoughts stretch out like pulled taffy.
>
> Consider Carter Hawley Hale Stores [a West coast retailer]. In its 1989 annual report, Chairman Philip Hawley wrote that the company was "laying the foundation for our profit growth in the 1990s." In 1990 the same thought fattened into this: "We are fully committed to accomplishing a major improvement in the profitability of this company in the current difficult retail environment." Two months later, Carter Hawley Hale filed [for bankruptcy].
>
> Or take Columbia Savings & Loan, the Beverly Hills thrift.... For 1987, when Columbia earned $119 million, the letter to shareholders from Chairman Abraham Spiegel and his son ... was 640 words long. For 1988, as earnings crashed to $65 million, the Spiegels' letter took 1,200 words....[1]

The reporters speculated that as a company's financial performance deteriorates over time, the verbosity in the firm's letter to stockholders increases.

■ DIRECTIONS

1. Obtain an annual report of a company whose performance has been marked by wide swings in prosperity over a short period of time. Examples may include many retailers, now-bankrupt airlines, failed banks, computer companies, energy-related companies, and so forth. Study the readability of the chairman's

---

[1] See "Windbag Theory," *Forbes* (August 3, 1992), p. 43.

letter (or the letter to the stockholders, if there is no chairman's letter). Examine such features as length of the letter, words per sentence, and word length. If possible, use a software program such as Grammatik, which may be available at your school.

2. Write a brief analysis of the writing style and readability of the letter to the stockholders.

3. Compare your analysis to the income statements included in the annual report. Does your conclusion provide evidence to support or oppose the "windbag theory?"

4. Use the accompanying form to conduct a peer review of a class-mate's analysis of the readability of a chairman's letter to the stockholders.

A. GENERAL INFORMATION

Name of company analyzed _____

Year of annual report _____

Number of times reviewer read the analysis   _____

B. SPECIFIC FEEDBACK (check items as appropriate)

Analysis submitted on time   _____

Personal pronouns avoided   _____

Spelling errors corrected on writer's paper   _____

Grammatical errors corrected on writer's paper   _____

Awkward phrases noted on writer's paper   _____

C. SUBJECTIVE FEEDBACK

On a scale of 1 (poor) to 7 (outstanding), how effective was the writer's

Writing style   _____

Evaluation of the letter to the stockholders   _____

D. COMMENTS

Strengths of the analysis _____

_____

_____

Weaknesses of the analysis _____

_____

_____

Partnerships: Are They a Dying Breed?

■ INTRODUCTION

Partnerships have several unique features, one of which is unlimited liability. If a business organized as a partnership experiences financial difficulties, the personal assets of the partners become at risk. Consider the plight of partnerships—the most common business form for accountants, lawyers, and other professionals—as reported by *The Wall Street Journal*:

> ... a slew of big court damage awards—totaling close to $1 billion against U.S. accountants and attorneys in the past year alone—is raising some doubts about whether the nation's once-dominant form of business organization can survive.
>
> [Recently], the prestigious accounting firm Price Waterhouse was hit by a record $338 million negligence award. An Arizona state court levied the award in favor of Standard Chartered PLC for negligence related to the accounting firm's audits of an Arizona bank before it was purchased by [Standard Chartered]. The award represents about three times Price Waterhouse's insurance coverage.
>
> Some negligence attorneys and Price Waterhouse competitors suggest the giant accounting firm could have real trouble staying afloat because its 950 partners may wind up paying $200 million or more out of their own pockets if courts uphold the award.[1]

■ DIRECTIONS

1. Obtain a copy of this article from your library and write a short critique (a critical evaluation of the authors' ideas and claims). In your critique, be sure to include a consideration of the following issues:
    a. What is the main theme of the article?
    b. Based on your general knowledge, do you believe that the authors make a valid case?
    c. What types of evidence are used to support the claims and conclusions?
2. Perform a peer review of one of your classmate's critiques. Use the accompanying form to record the results of your review.

---

[1] *The Wall Street Journal* (June 10, 1992), pp. A1, A6.

- ■ Student's name _____
- ■ Peer review of _____
- ■ Date _____
- ■ Section _____

A. GENERAL INFORMATION

Name of article critiqued _____

Source of article _____

Number of times reviewer read the critique _____

B. SPECIFIC FEEDBACK (check items as appropriate)

Critique submitted on time _____

Personal pronouns avoided _____

Spelling errors corrected on writer's paper _____

Grammatical errors corrected on writer's paper _____

Awkward phrases noted on writer's paper _____

C. SUBJECTIVE FEEDBACK

On a scale of 1 (poor) to 7 (outstanding), how effective was the writer's

Writing style _____

Evaluation of the article _____

D. COMMENTS

Strengths of the critique _____

_____

_____

Weaknesses of the critique _____

_____

_____

Quality: Is It Really Worth the Cost?

■ INTRODUCTION

Quality control and total quality management (TQM) are hot topics these days. Having a quality product can mean beating the competition and having a more profitable operation in terms of cost reductions (e.g., rework and spoilage) and added revenues. For many companies, quality is a compulsion. A *Washington Post* reporter, writing about the Mars candy company, observed:

> Perfection in tiny details like the M on the M&M or the squiggle on top of a chocolate bar is painstakingly pursued. Millions of M&Ms are rejected for sale every day because their M's missed the mark or their shells didn't glow like headlights. A pinhole in a single Snickers is cause to destroy an entire production run.[1]

The Malcolm Baldrige National Quality Awards are examples of the value of quality. An article recently published in *The Dallas Morning News* noted that the award brings winners major new contracts. Success, though, may be costly, as the following excerpts from the article show:

> After Cadillac won in 1990, General Motors launched a lavish advertising campaign that tooted its own horn so loudly that the Texas attorney general's office sued.... The company was fined $10,000 ... under the Deceptive Trade Practices Act in part because GM claimed the government had praised the cars themselves, not just the quality-control process.
> Wallace Co., a 1990 small business winner from Houston, filed for ... bankruptcy protection a year after winning. Chief executive John Wallace said other factors contributed to the bankruptcy, but he admits that management spent too many hours giving free quality seminars and not enough time pursuing customers. With 60 requests a day for information, Wallace executives spent much of their time telling other small businesses the secrets of their success even as the company was on the brink of financial failure. "You have a tremendous obligation to spread the news and try to help other people," Mr. Wallace said.[2]

■ DIRECTIONS

1. Compile a list of benefits and drawbacks (i.e., costs) associated with running a quality operation, whether it be service, merchandising, or manufacturing in nature. You may want to find

---

[1] From Joel Brenner's *Washington Post* article, "The World According to the Planet Mars," reprinted in *The Dallas Morning News* (April 19, 1992), pp. 1H, 2H, 5H, 7H.

[2] "For Award Winners, Celebrity Comes at a Price," *The Dallas Morning News* (October 15, 1992), pp. D1, D2.

an article about TQM or reference the topic in a cost accounting textbook.

2. Compare the lists in a class discussion, evaluating each item with respect to perception and creativity.

Hail to the Chief

■ INTRODUCTION

The United States has had a budget director since 1921. Yet, only recently (1991) did our country get its first chief financial officer (CFO). That lucky individual was Edward Mazur, controller of the new Office of Federal Financial Management—an office created as part of an act to eliminate fraud, waste, abuse, and mismanagement. As *Forbes* magazine reported:

> The job description calls for Mazur ... to oversee junior financial officers at 23 federal agencies. The goal: to improve internal controls, consolidate hundreds of accounting systems and produce audited financial statements from each agency. "My job," says Mazur, "is to ensure that agency CFOs are heard."
>
> They've already given Mazur quite an earful. Among the problems brought to his attention: anticipated Medicare overpayments of $600 million ...; 79 incompatible accounting systems at Housing & Urban Development; charges of $35 billion in excess inventory at the Defense Department; [and] a billion-dollar-a-year increase in student loan defaults at Education.[1]

■ DIRECTIONS

1. Form a team with two other people in your class. Go to the library and locate the most recent Budget of the United States. Find the section that details the guidelines for the Office of the Federal Financial Management and read the directives for the year. Prepare a brief summary of the mandates for the CFO, and include your team's assessment of the impacts that may result.
2. Your team should determine whether an office of financial management (or something comparable) exists for the municipality, the county, and the state in which your school is located. List the name of the agency and the person in charge.

---

[1] See "The Accountant as a Diplomat," *Forbes* (February 17, 1992), p. 148.

General Motors and Ford: A Contrast in Labor Costs

■ INTRODUCTION

In a study performed in cooperation with the big three automakers, James Harbour, a manufacturing consultant, recently reported that employment levels at domestic plants put General Motors (GM) at a $4 billion annual labor cost disadvantage to Ford. Harbour noted that GM would need to cut more than 70,000 blue-collar jobs in assembly and parts operations to eliminate the $795 per-car gap between the two firms. Among other findings:

> Ford has improved its assembly productivity by 36% since 1980, and some Ford plants have all but erased the productivity advantage enjoyed by Japanese auto makers…. Ford's Kansas City, Mo., car assembly plant has 2.37 workers for every car produced, on a par with Toyota's Georgetown, Ky., factory, Mr. Harbour said. The five most efficient Big Three truck assembly plants in North America all belong to Ford….
>
> GM has improved its assembly productivity by just 11% since 1980…. GM has 51% more people per vehicle produced in its domestic assembly plants than does Ford. While it's well known among auto industry analysts that GM lags behind Ford in manufacturing efficiency, the magnitude of the gap detailed by the Harbour study is striking. GM executives declared time and again during the past three years that they were adopting "synchronous" manufacturing methods to make their operations "lean." It appears, however, that these efforts yielded little improvement.[1]

■ DIRECTIONS

1. How did Mr. Harbour probably determine the number of workers for every car produced?
2. GM uses four major departments in its manufacturing process: assembly, metal stamping, engine manufacturing, and transmission. Devise a way to determine the total labor cost per car.
3. Understanding that tensions between GM and the United Auto Workers (UAW) union are high, what economic and financial arguments would you advance to help close the gap between GM and Ford?

---

[1] See "GM's Labor Cost Disadvantage to Ford Is Placed at $4 Billion a Year by Study," *The Wall Street Journal* (October 6, 1992), pp. A2, A6.

Give and They Shall Take

■ INTRODUCTION

In recent years, cities and states have been aggressively bidding for plant sites and foreign investment centers. The competition for business has resulted in major incentive programs designed to lure companies planning to relocate. The following excerpt from an article in *The Dallas Morning News* gives an idea about the efforts that some municipalities are making to attract company relocations.

> Twenty years ago, communities attracted industry by setting aside a tract of land, constructing sewer, electric and water lines to the "industrial park," and waiting for companies to arrive—what one expert calls the "build-it-and-they-will-come" philosophy of business recruitment.
>
> No more. In the last few years, communities have begun offering elaborate packages of incentives to distinguish their sales pitch from that of other towns and cities desperate to attract new jobs or hang on to old ones. In the process, the spiraling incentives competition has transformed recruitment into a high-stakes game of one-upsmanship....
>
> [Recently], Indianapolis won a wild competition for a new United Airlines maintenance center that will create at least 6,300 jobs directly, and 11,000 jobs indirectly. The cost to the city and the state of Indiana: a whopping $294.6 million in incentives. State officials estimate it will take 16 years to recover the investment....[1]

■ DIRECTIONS

1. Locate another article that discusses incentive plans used by other cities or local governments. Examples include Barcelona's hosting of the 1992 Summer Olympics, Atlanta's bid for the 1996 Summer Olympics, the closing of a General Motors plant in Ypsilanti, Michigan, or the location of a BMW plant outside of Greenville, South Carolina. There are numerous recent cases available for selection. Be sure to cite your article properly.
2. List the incentives offered to attract the business, specifically noting the costs involved in obtaining the industry expansion.
3. Describe the various methods that accountants and financial consultants would use in advising local governments about the extent of the concessions and incentives granted.

---

[1] "Ask and Your Company Shall Receive," *The Dallas Morning News* (February 4, 1992), pp. 1D, 6D, 7D.

PART 3

Role Plays, Simulations, and Field Studies

A Day in the Life…
Accounting and the Regulators
Source Documents Are the Source
Personal Financial Statements
Down on the Farm
Disaster
To Catch a Thief
Systems Engineering
Up in Smoke
Inquiring Minds
Organizing a Corporation
Manufacturing Elements
Reliable Products
Bombing Out at Clipper Stadium

A Day in the Life...

■ INTRODUCTION

Far from being "pencil-necked geeks" hunched over adding machines, accountants are professionals who must understand and integrate a wide variety of business topics. For example, accountants working in a chemical plant will need to have a working knowledge of chemistry and engineering from time to time. CPAs taking inventory on a cattle ranch will need to comprehend something about the livestock to be counted. Accountants working in hospitals will become proficient in using various medical terms and determining the cost of certain procedures. Working as an accountant means that a person will gain experience in many different industries or many separate departments.

■ DIRECTIONS

Your assignment is to interview a practicing accountant (public, private, or governmental/not-for-profit) in order to identify what might occur during a typical day. Use the accompanying form to gather basic data. In the interview, you should ask the accountant to describe one of the most unusual or challenging events ever experienced. The results of your interview will be communicated to the class.

■ Student's name _____   ■ Date _____
                                                      ■ Section _____

Individual interviewed   _____

Employer (company name)   _____

Position within the company   _____

Date and time of interview   _____

Method/length of interview   _____

Notes about a typical day   _____

_____

_____

_____

_____

_____

_____

_____

_____

_____

_____

_____

Most unusual experience   _____

_____

_____

_____

How this interview changed my perceptions of an accountant _____

_____

_____

Accounting and the Regulators

■ INTRODUCTION

In addition to the basic financial statements customarily prepared by an accountant, volumes of other data and reports must flow from a typical accounting system. Many reports are required by various regulatory authorities. This case has been designed so that you can develop an understanding of the role and scope of regulations in the modern business environment. In order to appreciate the degree of influence that regulators have on a particular business, some familiarity with the day-to-day operations of the business is necessary.

■ DIRECTIONS

To begin this project you should identify a business type that you are willing to study (e.g., a bank, a gas station, a doctor's office, a restaurant, or perhaps the place where you work). It will be helpful if you know an individual in a position of influence within that business, but a personal contact is not essential. Try to avoid situations where more than two other classmates use the same type of business. You should use the following form to gather basic data and interview a person who is familiar with the regulatory agencies that have jurisdiction over the business. An assessment should be made of the various reports and reporting periods that are applicable to each regulatory body. When you have completed the interview, be ready to report your findings to the rest of the class.

Individual interviewed   _____

Employer/Industry   _____

Position within the company   _____

Date and time of interview   _____

Method/length of interview   _____

Regulatory Agency	**Type of Report**	**Reporting Period**
_____	_____	_____
_____	_____	_____
_____	_____	_____
_____	_____	_____
_____	_____	_____
_____	_____	_____
_____	_____	_____
_____	_____	_____
_____	_____	_____
_____	_____	_____
_____	_____	_____
_____	_____	_____
_____	_____	_____
_____	_____	_____
_____	_____	_____

Source Documents Are the Source

■ INTRODUCTION

You know that debits and credits entered into an accounting system must be triggered by a transaction or event. Further, a transaction (or event) is usually documented by some physical evidence. For example, a sales invoice might trigger the recording of a sale on account, or a deposit ticket might trigger the recording of a cash receipt.

A source document is also an important component of internal control. Poorly designed source documents can cause significant errors or even defalcations. Because source documents are so important to an accounting system, they are also vital to the success of a business.

■ DIRECTIONS

1. In your personal life you may have access to many source documents that serve as the entry points for some business's accounting system. Obtain (with permission) one or more samples of a source document and bring them to class for a discussion and comparison.

2. After reviewing several source documents, you will have an appreciation for their importance. Use the following information to design an appropriate source document.

   Your neighbor, Fred Glines, is a master craftsman who has generated a prospering business, "Custom Kitchens." He custom designs and then constructs cabinets for new and remodeled kitchens. Most of his customers are contractors, but he has many private customers as well.

   He has come to you for advice. Lately, he has been "stuck" with large bad debts from a few customers who have ordered work, paid a $100 deposit, and then defaulted or changed their minds. Fred is so busy with cabinet making that he is having trouble tracking the customers and their deposits. You have agreed to help him one day each week.

   a. First, advise Fred how he can minimize his problems with customers changing their minds.

   b. Design a source document that Fred can use to record his orders for the week so that you can follow-up and record the deposits and receivables.

Personal Financial Statements

■ INTRODUCTION

On the balance sheets of most businesses, assets and liabilities are reported using the historical-cost principle, and the related fair market values (what the items are "worth") are not disclosed. Even though historical cost is both objective and verifiable, many people question the relevance of such amounts for decision making. Nonetheless, historical cost is the basis for financial reporting for all but a few cases.

One exception is when banks ask individuals for their personal financial statements. The banks usually require the use of fair market value instead of historical cost for assets and liabilities reported. Because of this reporting difference, the terminology pertaining to personal financial statements is slightly different. Personal balance sheets are called *statements of financial condition*.

■ DIRECTIONS

Use the following form to prepare your own statement of financial condition. When listing your assets and liabilities, be sure to adhere to the proper definitions of assets and liabilities. Do not include dollar balances on the statement that you turn in to your instructor.

Your name _____

Statement of Financial Condition

Date _____

Assets		**Liabilities**	
Cash	$ _____	_____	$ _____
_____	_____	_____	_____
_____	_____	_____	_____
_____	_____	_____	_____
_____	_____	_____	_____
_____	_____	_____	_____
_____	_____	_____	_____
_____	_____	_____	_____
_____	_____	_____	_____
_____	_____	_____	_____
_____	_____	_____	_____
_____	_____	_____	_____
_____	_____	_____	_____
Total	$ _____	Total	$ _____

What do you think the difference between your assets and your liabilities should be called?

Down on the Farm

■ INTRODUCTION

Tom Todd has just completed his first year as a cotton farmer. During the past 12 months, he has leased a farm and the necessary equipment that he needed. Because he thoroughly enjoyed his experience, he has decided to pursue a farming career full time. To do this, he needs to buy land and equipment.

Todd met Martha Delle, a loan officer at the Farmers Bank and Trust, about financing his purchases. He took a small notebook that he had kept during the 12 months he had been farming. Delle examined the notebook and returned it to Todd, indicating politely that his records needed to be formalized before she could evaluate his business for a loan application.

Relevant excerpts from Todd's notebook include:

Jan.   2   *Today I contacted Otto Hanna and leased his 100-acre farm. We agreed that I would pay him one-fourth of the gross proceeds from the sale of my cotton. The crop is to be sold as soon as possible after harvest.*

        5   *I opened a bank account for the farm and deposited $20,000.*

        8   *Went to town and bought fertilizer that cost $2,400; also rented a tractor from the fertilizer dealer for $900. I paid one-half of the total amount due and agreed to pay the remaining balance later.*

        9   *Fuel for the tractor cost $80; paid in cash.*

     15   *Went to town to return the tractor, paid the balance owed to the fertilizer dealer. While in town I wrote a $65 check on the farm's bank account to pay for family groceries.*

Mar.   1   *Bought cotton seed for $480 (a new hybrid kind) and rented a tractor and planter for $1,200; paid in full.*

        4   *Returned the tractor. Fuel cost another $640 (cash).*

July   29   *No rain again — 65 days and still counting.*

Aug.   27   *Had the cotton sprayed in preparation for harvest (cost $1,800). The sprayer company gave extended terms — don't have to pay until the end of next month.*

Sept.   4   *Harvest day — finally!! I paid the crew $1,480.*

     16   *The cotton was processed today. Received $300 per bale, only 30 bales were produced. Extremely disappointing results, primarily because of the summer drought. Plan to pay the proper amount to Otto in a week.*

     23   *Settled my obligation with Otto, balance due, $0.*

Nov.   1   *Mailed a check to the spraying company. I had almost forgotten, until a phone call today.*

Dec.   18   *Reached a decision to buy my own farm next year.*

■ DIRECTIONS

1. Specify the components of a simplified accounting system that Todd could use to process transactions for his farm. Include a chart of accounts, with account numbers.

2. Use the system you just suggested to record and process the farm's transactions for the year. (Hint: Hanna's share of the sale proceeds should be recorded as a liability of the farm and should not be treated as farm revenue.)

3. Prepare a trial balance and comment on the success or failure of the first year of operation.

4. Assume that you are Delle. Should Todd's application for a loan be approved?

Disaster

■ INTRODUCTION

This case gives you an opportunity to anticipate your actions in the event of a forecasted disaster. Proper preparations can sometimes make the difference between the survival and failure of a business affected by a catastrophe. Unfortunately, many disasters—such as fires, tornadoes, or earthquakes—give no early warnings. However, if you and your business have an adequate internal control system (which should include precautionary measures for calamities), you will be able to prevent much unnecessary loss.

■ DIRECTIONS

You are the office manager of a large veterinary clinic on the coast. A major hurricane, hovering in the ocean, has suddenly turned its course and is headed directly toward your city. Expected landfall is in six hours. This is a class-four hurricane, and its damage is expected to be similar to the havoc left by Hurricanes Hugo and Andrew. The governor has ordered the immediate evacuation of the entire coastal area.

You have taken care of your personal business and are on your way out of town. Before you leave, you need to spend some time at the clinic making sure that you do all that is possible to prepare for the storm.

When you arrive, you discover that the vets have already moved the animals and are working together to secure the windows and the doors. You think that they are taking reasonable precautions concerning the physical protection of the premises.

You estimate that you have only 30 minutes to take care of your responsibilities as manager of the business. What steps and measures will you take, assuming the worst-case scenario?

To Catch a Thief

■ INTRODUCTION

Internal control is one of the most important concepts that you will learn in accounting. Safeguarding assets and adhering to managerial goals will be significant considerations in your life no matter what career you choose. An appreciation of internal control systems will help you to be a better manager, a more successful entrepreneur, or a better employee. Developing a sense of internal control in your day-to-day activities may even save you money. (As proof of that point, how often have you received the wrong order or incorrect change at a fast-food drive-through?)

■ DIRECTIONS

This assignment involves your assessment of **any** internal control system. It could be a bank, a parking garage, a store, a cafeteria food line, or your school's registration system, for example. You should observe the system, look for the existing controls, and identify a weakness. In a way, you will be thinking like a thief. Consider the way the controls could be circumvented and then determine a corrective action. Use the accompanying form to record your observations and suggestions.

■ Student's name _____   ■ Date _____

                                                  ■ Section _____

Date of observation   _____

Description of the system observed _____

_____

_____

Brief list of existing controls   _____

_____

_____

_____

_____

_____

_____

Weaknesses or possibilities of circumvention   _____

_____

_____

_____

_____

_____

Suggestions for improvement _____

_____

_____

_____

_____

Systems Engineering

■ INTRODUCTION

In this case, you will be asked to design and implement a computerized accounting system. You will work on one of four teams. Since this project may take several weeks to complete, you may want to choose teammates who have schedules and locations that are convenient to yours.

The four teams are:

Team 1   Systems Design
Team 2   Programming
Team 3   Control and Debugging
Team 4   User Group

The accounting system to be designed is for the use of Tom Todd, the farmer in the case Down on the Farm. Before beginning this case, be sure that you are familiar with the other.

■ DIRECTIONS

Team 1—Systems Design

This team will decide how the accounting system should function. Their plans should include as much detail as possible, including flow charts, narrative descriptions, pictorial displays of desired output, etc. After considering all aspects of the system's design, they should meet with the program team to communicate their plans.

Team 2—Programming

This team ideally should be comprised of students who are generally familiar with the operations of an electronic spreadsheet package. This group must develop an electronic spreadsheet program that will implement the vision of the system design team. The programming team may need to reapproach the design team with proposed modifications, simplifications, and discussion of other problems encountered during programming. Once the program is completed to the satisfaction of the programming team, it will be passed to the control and debugging team.

Team 3—Control and Debugging

This team will be responsible for evaluating the program for suitability, testing it for potential transactions, and returning it to the programming team for suggested revisions and modifications as necessary. A concern of this group is that the program be user-friendly and accessible to individuals without a detailed knowledge of accounting.

Team 4—User Group

The final team will invent a sample set of transactions for Tom Todd's next three months of operations. They will attempt to account for the transactions using the program that was developed. The results of their efforts should be financial statements that Todd will present to the bank.

Up in Smoke

■ INTRODUCTION

R.J. Reynolds Tobacco (RJRT, for short) is an operating unit of RJR Nabisco, Inc., one of the world's largest consumer products companies. Presented below are excerpts from a note in one of its recent annual reports.

> Various legal actions, proceedings and claims are pending or may be instituted ... including those claiming that lung cancer and other diseases have resulted from the use of or exposure to RJRT's tobacco products .... The plaintiffs in these actions seek recovery .... In two recent smoking and health cases in which neither RJRT nor any affiliate ... was a party ... juries have found in favor of plaintiffs. Determinations of liability or adverse rulings against other cigarette manufacturers ... could adversely affect the litigation against RJRT ... and increase the number of such claims.

■ DIRECTIONS

You will be assigned to one of three teams that will research this issue and be ready to discuss it at a simulated meeting of RJR Nabisco's stockholders. The teams are (1) management; (2) the accountants for RJR's auditing firm; and (3) stockholders.

Stockholders' Team

Stockholders with questions generally use the stockholders' meeting as their forum. Disgruntled stockholders especially will make efforts to be present to question management about policies and strategies. However, all members of this team need not be hostile. Some stockholders should support the sales of tobacco. As part of your assignment, write a question to the auditors about the financial consequences of the above note.

Management Team

Your team will govern the stockholders' meeting. Choose the team members who will be the speakers at the meeting. Remember that your job is to be positive and enthusiastic about the company, but be ready to defend yourself against hostile stockholders. Consider using the annual reports of other tobacco companies or hazardous industries in your defense. Be creative in your resources.

Auditor's Team

Be prepared to explain the accounting treatment regarding the above note and other questions that may arise in the meeting. Determine whether a liability should be reported on the balance sheet.

Inquiring Minds

■ INTRODUCTION

Very often an accountant or businessperson will need to gather a variety of facts, figures, and other information by verbal inquiry of others. These inquiries must be carefully constructed to gather the information desired in an efficient and effective manner. In addition, care should be exercised to avoid redundant or incomplete questions. It is also important to assume a professional but congenial attitude in order not to annoy the respondent. Additionally, questioners should condition themselves to listen carefully to all responses.

■ DIRECTIONS

Two teams will participate in this role-playing exercise. Team 1 will conduct an interview of Team 2. **Read the information below that applies to your team only.** After the preparation time allotted by your instructor, conduct the interview, which should not last longer than five minutes. The results of the interview will be an aging of accounts receivable and any necessary adjusting entries.

Team 1 Requirements

You are to gather enough information in the questioning process to prepare an aging of accounts receivable and determine the appropriate adjusting entry needed at year-end. You cannot ask the same question twice, and you have only five minutes to gather the information that is needed. You may find it helpful to draft an aging schedule in preparation for your interview. Based upon the data you gather from your inquiries, prepare any necessary adjusting entries.

Team 2 Requirements

In responding to the questions that are directed to you, use the data below to answer honestly and specifically, but do not provide any information that is not requested directly and explicitly. In other words, when the inquiring team asks a question, do not volunteer any information.

You should also prepare any adjusting entries that you believe are necessary. List suggestions that would have improved Team 1's inquiry.

Accounts Receivable Data

At the end of the current accounting period, the company has total accounts receivable of $1,242,000. Of this amount, $27,000 is definitely uncollectible and should be written off prior to preparing an aging of accounts receivable. Of the remaining receivables, half are less than 30 days old, and 2 percent of this amount is estimated to be uncollectible. Forty percent of the remaining receivables are 31 to 60 days old, and 90 percent of these are estimated to be collectible. The rest of the receivables are older than 61 days and are expected to be 60 percent uncollectible. The allowance for uncollectible accounts receivable currently has a $50,000 balance. However, this is a debit balance because of excessive write-offs that were necessitated during the most recent accounting period.

Calculations for Team 2:

Organizing a Corporation

■ INTRODUCTION

Given that 19.4 percent of the firms in the United States produce 90.2 percent of the country's business receipts, the corporate form of organization clearly dominates our economy in monetary terms. Corporations are often considered preferable for conducting business affairs, and many proprietorships and partnerships choose to change to the corporate form.

■ DIRECTIONS

You and your group will form a corporation in this exercise. You may determine the nature and name of your business. Elect an unofficial ("incorporating") board of directors to begin. (A real board cannot be elected until the corporation has been formed.) Have the chair delegate the following duties. Some tasks are more involved than others, so more "team-power" will be needed for them. Ask the board members to report on their findings at the next meeting.

1. List the advantages and disadvantages of the corporate form.
2. Use your library to find information about organizing a corporation in your state.
    a. Prepare a flow chart of the major steps involved in forming a corporation in your state.
    b. Attempt to find a model set of articles of incorporation that would be minimally sufficient for forming a corporation.
    c. Call an attorney or the Secretary of State's office for information if your library research proves fruitless.
3. Using the information obtained from the research, modify the articles to include specifics decided by your board: class(es) of stock to issue, existence of preemptive rights, par versus no-par stock and any related amounts, number of shares to authorize, conversion features, etc.
4. Fill in the accompanying corporate certificate using the results of your board meetings.

SHARES

NUMBER

4L67

INCORPORATED UNDER THE LAWS OF

THE STATE OF _____

This Certifies that _____

of $ _____ Par Value each of the _____ Capital Stock of

_____ is the owner of

_____ Shares

transferable only on the books of the Corporation by the holder hereof in person or by Attorney upon surrender of this Certificate properly endorsed.

IN WITNESS WHEREOF, the said Corporation has caused this certificate to be signed by its duly authorized officers and to be sealed with the seal of the Corporation dated _____

_____
AUTHORIZED SIGNATURE

_____
PRESIDENT

Manufacturing Elements

■ **INTRODUCTION**

Your textbook explains that the three ingredients in work in process are raw materials, direct labor, and overhead. Several examples of familiar operations are used in the textbook presentation to help you visualize the process and to understand overhead application. If you have ever visited a factory, your ability to perceive these components is magnified. This case gives you an opportunity to become familiar with a manufacturing operation in your vicinity.

■ **DIRECTIONS**

Identify a local manufacturing concern in your area and interview a cost accountant (or other knowledgeable individual in the accounting department) to determine the following information for the company. Use the accompanying form and be prepared to report your results as part of a class discussion.

Individual interviewed   _____

Employer (company name)   _____

Position within the company   _____

Date and time of interview   _____

Method/length of interview   _____

Products manufactured   _____

                                _____

                                _____

Direct materials   _____

                                _____

                                _____

Indirect materials   _____

                                _____

                                _____

Other elements of overhead   _____

                                _____

                                _____

Overhead allocation methods   _____

                                _____

                                _____

                                _____

Reliable Products

■ INTRODUCTION

You have recently accepted a new job in the accounting department of Reliable Products. After only one week of employment, you found the following memo on your desk. It is from Pat Willis, your supervisor.

Due to a death in the family, I will be gone for 10 days. As you know, I've been working on a project concerning Reliable's overhead application rates. Because the project must be completed shortly after my return, I need some assistance. Specifically, you should focus on two issues. First, should overhead rates be changed every quarter to correspond with our highly seasonal business? Second, should each department set individual overhead rates in view of the significant differences that exist among departmental operations?

I know that these issues might be a little difficult to understand given that you've only been here one week and you had very little cost accounting while in school. Try your best and have recommendations on my desk by the time I return. I've attached the following material for further information. Thanks.

Pat

A. Quarterly Overhead Rates

As you know, our business is highly seasonal. Because of a lack of competition for many of our products, cost is a major factor in determining selling price. The following figures are for item number 8872, a representative product.

| | Quarter | | | |
	1	2	3	4
Production (units)	5,000	20,000	8,000	25,000
Direct materials	$ 25,000	$100,000	$ 40,800	$127,500
Direct labor	40,000	160,000	65,600	205,000
Variable factory overhead	10,000	40,000	16,000	52,500
Fixed factory overhead	100,000	100,000	100,000	100,000
Total cost	$175,000	400,000	222,400	$485,000
Cost per unit	$35	$20	$27.80	$19.40
Overhead per unit	$22	$ 7	$14.50	$ 6.10

B. Departmental Rates

We have two primary departments: Machining and Assembly. The Machining Department uses very costly, intricate equipment in manufacturing various products. The resulting depreciation and power costs are high. Upon completion, goods are passed from Machining to Assembly. In the Assembly Department there is a limited amount of equipment, because the emphasis is on manual labor. A sampling of recent jobs revealed this data.

	Hours Spent In		
Job No.	Machining	Assembly	Total
431	28	4	32
432	5	30	35
433	18	50	68
434	30	10	40

As you can see, there can be considerable variation among jobs. At present a single, plantwide overhead rate is used for product costing.

■ DIRECTIONS

Use the information to write a report for Pat in memo form. Despite the casual tone of Pat's memo, yours must be more formal because it will likely be used by upper management. In your report, consider at least the following three factors: (1) whether Reliable should change its selling price each quarter to correspond with the unit cost change, (2) the primary cause behind the fluctuating unit costs and what might be done to alleviate the problem, and (3) a recommendation concerning the use of a single, combined overhead rate for all departments.

Your report should discuss your recommendations, but does not need to include your computations. If you prepare worksheets to help you analyze the information, you may refer to them in your memo and assume that they would be attached to your report. In other words, this memo should be a written description of your conclusions, not a compilation of your calculations.

Bombing Out at Clipper Stadium

■ INTRODUCTION

Clipper Investment Group owns and operates a stadium used by the Bombers baseball team. For each game during the baseball season, which extends from April through the end of September, Clipper must employ 300 people to handle food concessions, ticket sales, program/novelty sales, and general cleaning and maintenance. The Bombers play 82 home games on 63 dates (the difference being due to double-headers). Employees are paid $20 for a single game and $35 for a double-header. Few employees work more than two months, and total earnings are subject to all payroll and unemployment taxes.

Close supervision is exercised over all employees. Fifteen supervisors are paid $1,000 per month. Additionally, Clipper pays for insurance for all employees and supervisors at an annual cost of $120 per person. All stadium personnel are permitted to eat at the ball park for 30 percent of the posted prices (which approximates the actual food cost). Finally, employees are furnished with uniforms, which they are not required to return. Clipper spent $12,000 on uniforms last year, but the uniform manufacturer has recently announced a 10 percent price increase for the upcoming season.

A temporary personnel company called People Power has proposed to staff the facility (including supervisors) at a yearly cost of $655,000. As part of the proposal, People Power will pay all employees and will cover all payroll tax expense and insurance. Clipper is strongly considering this proposal because the present personnel turnover is high, and employee processing is consuming a large amount of staff time. Clipper would need to provide uniforms and continue the present food policy. Management estimates that the personnel office should save $10,000 in processing costs if the outside service is used.

■ DIRECTIONS

You will be assigned to participate as a member of one of three groups: (1) management, (2) staff in favor of People Power's proposal, and (3) staff opposed to the change. Each staff team (groups 2 and 3) should prepare a presentation to management to argue its position. In class, the staff teams will make their respective presentations of no longer than 10 minutes each. The management group will make the final decision, clearly stating why their conclusion was reached.

PART 4

Innovative Challenges

An Accounting Journal for Students

■ INTRODUCTION

One of the goals of your principles of accounting course is to improve your communication skills. Many of the cases and exercises in this book have been prepared with that goal in mind. Research has found that another effective way to enhance communication and to reinforce technical concepts is to keep a journal. A journal is separate and distinct from your class notes, and will be a means for one-on-one communication between you and your instructor.

Your journal can be used in two different ways. First, you can use your journal during class, separately from your notes, to summarize main ideas that have been discussed. For example, after having discussed the entity assumption in class, your instructor might ask you to describe the concept in your journal. An example of a response to this request would be:

> The entity assumption states that economic events can be identified with a particular unit of accountability. This assumption requires that the activities of the entity be kept separate and apart from the activities of the owner or other businesses.

Second, your journal will be used outside of class as correspondence with your instructor. You are encouraged to express concerns and ask questions about the course or specific topics. For example, you may find an ambiguous paragraph in your class notes that makes you wonder if you really understand a certain topic. You have reviewed your class notes and referenced the book, but you are still unsure. You should express your concern in your journal.

The following two entries were taken from actual, recent student journals. One student wrote:

> Adjustments I can handle, but I'm still having a little trouble with closing entries and the post-closing trial balance. Are all revenues and expenses left off the post-closing trial balance? I understand the income summary or how to do it in the closing entries.

Another student wrote:

> I really appreciate your help on the computer problem last week. Although I didn't get it done in time to turn it in for credit, my mind was at ease because I finally understand the problem.

In these cases, as should be the case for all questions and comments, the instructor responded to each remark.

■ **DIRECTIONS**

Obtain two blue books for this assignment. Once a week you will exchange blue books with your instructor. Having two books means that you will always have a book to write in while your instructor is responding to your last entries in the other book.

Remember that the journal is for your benefit, and you will profit from the journal if you spend some time thinking about what you do or do not understand.

Testing 1, 2, 3

■ INTRODUCTION

One of the best ways to review for a test or exam is to write your own test questions. Examining the material from the instructor's perspective gives you a totally different view of the topics. Often, in writing a question, you will discover aspects of a subject that you may have missed.

If your instructor uses multiple-choice questions on tests, this assignment is an excellent way to improve your objective testing skills. Even if your tests do not include multiple choice questions, writing some will help you to learn and reevaluate the material. You will be amazed at the benefits of this exercise.

■ DIRECTIONS

Start by writing two multiple choice questions for each chapter. Try to make one question conceptual and the other computational. Use four answer choices, A through D. Avoid using "None of the above" as one of the answer choices. Make sure that you write unambiguous questions that you can solve.

You can share your questions with members of your study group as preparation for a test. Additionally, your instructor may ask you to turn in some of your questions, so be sure that your questions are legible.

Please Hire Me

■ INTRODUCTION

You have just learned that an amusement park in your area wants to hire a summer intern for its accounting department. In addition to a generous salary and good experience, the intern will receive two free passes to the park for the summer. You have decided that you would really like to have this job.

Your overall grade point average is not the greatest, but you have done fairly well in your business courses. You believe that if you can get the park to give you an interview, you will be able to use your personality and communication skills to persuade them to hire you. In order to get an interview, you and all the other applicants must write a letter and send your resume to the personnel director, Raphael Barredo.

■ DIRECTIONS

Write a cover letter to the personnel director. Design your own letterhead and layout. Introduce yourself in the first paragraph and describe your qualifications in the second paragraph. Use the third paragraph creatively to convince the director to see you. The last paragraph should be a summary and closing.

You will write many letters like this over the course of your life. Use this opportunity to practice selling yourself in a persuasive and professional manner.

Is This Accounting or High School Arithmetic?[1]

■ INTRODUCTION

Most students enter their first accounting class with the notion that they must be very proficient in math. They soon learn that accounting involves more arithmetic than math—in other words, there is more addition and subtraction than algebra or calculus. With the use of a calculator, students do not usually have much difficulty with the "mathematical" aspects of accounting.

Nonetheless, American students are often criticized for their weakening math skills. The following questions appeared on arithmetic tests given in June 1885 to prospective high school students in Jersey City, New Jersey. Could you have worked these problems in high school? Remember, there were no calculators in 1885!

■ DIRECTIONS

See if you can answer each of the following questions using some of the accounting principles and practices you have studied.

1. If a 60-day note of $840 is discounted at a bank at 4.5 percent, what are the proceeds?

    _____

    _____

2. The interest on $50 from March 1st to July 1st is $2.50. What is the rate?

    _____

    _____

3. What is the cost of 1,983 pounds of sugar at $98.50 a ton?

    _____

    _____

---

[1] Excerpted from the *Wall Street Journal*, June 9, 1992.

4. The masonwork on a building can be finished by 16 men in 24 days working 10 hours a day. How long will it take 22 men working 8 hours a day?

_____

_____

5. A merchant sold a quantity of goods for $18,775. He deducts 5 percent for cash and then finds that he has made 10 percent. What did he pay for the goods?

_____

_____

6. By selling goods at 12.5 percent profit a man clears $800. What was the cost of the goods, and for what were they sold?

_____

_____

7. A merchant offered some goods for $1,170.90 cash, or $1,206 payable in 30 days. Which was the better offer for the customer, money being worth 10 percent?

_____

_____

Roommate Dialogue

■ **INTRODUCTION**

The purpose of this exercise is to reflect about your experiences as a student in accounting principles.

■ **DIRECTIONS**

Complete the following dialogue based on your experiences in accounting principles during this term.

Your roommate, taking a break from studying for a final exam, asks you about your accounting class: "How did accounting go this semester? I know you dreaded taking it. Did it turn out to be as awful as you thought?"

Your reply: _____

_____

_____

_____

_____

_____

_____

_____

_____

_____

_____

_____

_____

_____

_____

Your roommate is not in the mood to study and is not satisfied with your answer. The questioning continues: "Well, what was the most important thing you learned in accounting? How do you think it will it help you in your career? Do you think it would help me, even though I'm a history major? My math skills are not very good, you know."

Your reply: _____

_____

_____

_____

_____

_____

_____

_____

_____

Your roommate is thinking that maybe accounting will be a good elective. Sensing your exasperation, a final question is presented: "You've survived this course. Can you give me any tips or suggestions that will help me when I take it?"

You respond: "Sure, I've got several hints that I wish someone had told me before I started this course. I'll tell you some right now, but then you've got to let me study!"

_____

_____

_____

_____

_____

_____

_____

Crossword Puzzle Review 1
(Introduction through Partnerships)

Across

1 An intangible asset representing rights that authorize the manufacture or sale of certain products

3 Cash _____: offered to credit customers to encourage prompt payment of invoices

4 An act, commonly called Social Security

7 The termination of a partnership's life

10 _____ assets lack physical substance

11 _____ sheet: a financial statement

13 _____ price: basic catalogue price for merchandise

16 The allocation of the cost of intangible assets to the accounting periods benefited

17 A complete reporting of all financially important facts

20 _____ occurs when all temporary account balances are transferred to owner's equity

22 A business formed by two or more persons

24 An agency of the U.S. Treasury Department

27 The initials of one of the textbook's authors

28 A characteristic of financial information that fairly depicts the conditions it purports to present

30 Federal legislation that requires employers to pay taxes to assist the unemployed

31 A debt that is owed by an enterprise

32 A computerized listing that shows the various program options available to a user

34 _____ assumption states that a business is viewed separately from its owners

35 A customer's check returned by the bank

36 _____ balance: type of balance usually found in a ledger account

37 A chronological record that serves as an entry point for transactions

Down

1 _____ year: any one-year period other than a calendar year

2 A national organization of licensed CPAs

5 _____ accounts receivable: segregation of individual accounts based on the length of time outstanding

6 An exclusive right that permits its owner to use, manufacture, and sell a product or process

7 The allocation process of natural resource cost

8 A rise in the general price level that causes a decline in the purchasing power of the dollar

9 Current _____: a measure of liquidity

12 _____ expenses are unpaid and matched against revenues under the accrual basis

14 An error that occurs when two digits of a given number have been reversed

15 A charge made for the use of borrowed funds

18 _____ principle stipulates that entities employ the same accounting practices in each reporting period

19 The process used to allocate the cost of long-lived assets to the accounting periods benefited

20 The right-hand side of a T-account

21 Amounts that a business expects to collect from claims against customers

23 The amount on which interest is computed

25 The process by which the transactions in a journal are transferred to the ledger

26 Amounts charged customers for goods sold or services rendered

27 How close an asset is to becoming cash

29 Goods acquired for resale to customers

32 The one that promises to pay the stipulated amount of a note

33 An inventory accounting method based on the premise that costs are matched against revenues in reverse order of occurrence

Crossword Puzzle Review 1

make or puzzle students have make one.

Crossword Puzzle Review 2
(Corporations through Managerial)

Across

2   A negative balance in retained earnings
4   A document related to new stock issues and required by the SEC
8   _____ overhead: a situation arising when the factory overhead applied to production is greater than the amount actually incurred
11 Cost _____: a factor that causes given costs to be incurred within an organization
12 Bond _____: difference between the face value of bonds and the issue price when issuance occurs above face value
15 Inventory of goods started but not completed during the period (abbreviation)
18 Padding used in budgeting to avoid unfavorable appraisals
19 _____ cost: contains both fixed and variable elements
20 Widely used profitability ratio (abbreviation)
23 _____ unit: physical unit stated in terms of a finished unit
24 A company that has another company as its majority stockholder
28 _____ analysis: calculation of dollar and percentage changes for corresponding items in comparative financial statements
29 Distributions of income by a corporation to its stockholders
31 Component of a company whose activities represent a major line of business or class of customer
33 Deviations from a budget or standard
34 _____ range: area of activity where a cost relationship is expected to hold true
35 _____ cost: differs among alternatives
37 Supplemental, yet integral, part of financial statements
38 _____ of retained earnings: separation of retained earnings account to inform financial statement readers that a portion of the account is unavailable for dividend distribution
39 Norm used by businesses to measure what should occur under reasonably efficient operating conditions
40 _____ - _____ point: level of activity where revenues and expenses are equal, and net income is zero
41 _____ ratio: severe measure of short-term debt-paying ability that relates the total of cash, short-term investments, and accounts receivable to total current liabilities

Down

1 Formal quantitative expression of management expectations generated for any area that is deemed critical

3 _____ budget: covers a range of activity as opposed to a single level

5 _____ method: type of analysis that measures the amount of time necessary to recover a project's initial cash investment

6 A state-issued document that provides evidence of business incorporation

7 _____ cost: direct materials used plus direct labor

9 _____ cost: any cost that is easily traced to and associated with a business segment

10 Stock _____: agreements with investors to purchase stock at a given price, with payment taking place on a future date

13 _____ materials: items to be processed into salable goods

14 Process of taking a future amount and bringing it back to its value today

16 _____ center: responsibility unit in which a manager is evaluated on profit and the effective use of assets

17 Management by _____: practice of focusing a manager's attention on those aspects of operations that deviate from planned results

21 Factory _____: all factory-related costs other than prime costs

22 A company that is the majority owner of another company

24 _____ budget: developed for one level of activity

25 _____ cost: cost that varies in direct proportion to a change in an activity base

26 Agreement allowing one party to use the assets of another party for a stated period of time

27 _____ costs: costs incurred to establish a corporation

30 _____ report: designed to provide the manager of a responsibility center with timely feedback of operating results

32 _____ note: long-term note issued to finance the purchase of real estate

36 _____ bond: bond by which specific assets are pledged as security for the bondholders

39 _____ cost: a past cost that is irrelevant for decision making

Crossword Puzzle Review 2

Word Power[1]

■ INTRODUCTION

The following "Word Power" appeared in the *Reader's Digest* and was presented as a banking exercise, but you will see how many of the terms were introduced in your accounting course.

■ DIRECTIONS

It Pays to Enrich Your Word Power
By Peter Funk

"To bank or not to bank, *that* is the question" for many people wondering what to do with their savings. The following words come from various press commentaries on the banking industry's difficulties. How many of these words can you "bank" on? Mark the answer you think is correct.

1. **consolidate** *v.*—A: to complete. B: distribute. C: combine. D: offer.
2. **legal tender** *n.*—A: laundered money. B: intrabank transaction. C: legitimate currency. D: credit.
3. **arrears** (ah REARZ) *n.*—A: privileged knowledge. B: missing inventory. C: extended loan. D: unpaid, overdue debt.
4. **mature** *adj.*—A: past due. B: excessive. C: inactive. D: payable.
5. **promissory note** *n.*—A: written promise. B: mortgage. C: stock certificate. D: favorable loan.
6. **roll over** *v.*—A: to refinance. B: relax laws. C: negotiate favorably. D: be passive.
7. **point** *n.*—A: lease. B: bonus to borrower. C: late-payment penalty. D: prepaid interest.
8. **redundant** *adj.*—A: scarce. B. overabundant. C: increasing. D: stagnant.
9. **demand deposit** *n.*—A: short-term loan. B: mortgage payment. C: checking account. D: reinvestment of interest.
10. **voucher** *n.*—A: document proving payment. B: statement of financial condition. C: account book. D: withdrawal of money.
11. **convertible** *adj.*—A: inconsistent. B: exchangeable. C: shoddy. D: collectible.
12. **liquid assets** *n.*—valuables that are A: of a floating value. B: volatile. C: suddenly worthless. D: in cash.
13. **debacle** *n.*—A: complication. B: trickery. C: evil. D: collapse.
14. **par value** *n.*—A: face amount. B: average cost. C: market equivalent. D: worth at sale.

---

[1] Reprinted with permission from the August 1991 *Reader's Digest*. Copyright 1991 by the Reader's Digest Assn., Inc.

15. **conveyance** *n.*—A: compromise. B: legal brief. C: property survey. D: deed.
16. **ire** (EYE 'r) *n.*—A: pride. B: pity. C: determination. D: anger.
17. **lien** (LEAN) *n.*—A: legal claim. B: false statement. C: stock offering. D: sales invoice.
18. **compound interest** *n.*—interest paid on A: principal. B: bonds. C: principal and unpaid interest. D: stocks.
19. **fungible** (FUN juh b'l) *adj.*—A: expendable. B: interchangeable. C: dated. D: mildewed.
20. **sacred cow** *n.*—anything thought of as A: above criticism. B: unusual. C: well-heeled. D: showy or pompous.

MGM: Make a Great Movie

■ INTRODUCTION

The proliferation of video recorders has turned millions of Americans into amateur movie producers. In addition to recording family events or memorable moments, a production of a video can be a useful learning experience.

■ DIRECTIONS

Work in groups or as a class. Borrow a camcorder from a willing lender or use one from your school's audio/visual resource center. Your assignment is to produce a 10- to 15-minute video about an accounting topic or scenario. You can use one of the role plays or simulations presented in this book as a basis, or you can decide on another situation, such as a job interview. You can conduct an interview with an accountant or film a manufacturing plant tour. The possibilities are wide open.

You may choose and write your own script. Make the presentation enjoyable, but your video should be informative rather than amusing. Your video may be used in future accounting classes.

This project should be well planned and professionally conceptualized. Improvisation and ad libbing while filming will detract from the value of the video. Therefore, the effort may take several meetings to develop before filming, so don't wait until the last minute.

West Accounting Trivia Game Instructions[1]

Objectives Related to the Course
1. Review the course material covered in Accounting Principles
2. Get to know other students in the class
3. Develop a system of fair play
4. Have fun

Equipment
In addition to the game board and questions that are included in this book, players will need:

—one die
—a game marker (or coin) for each player
—a score sheet for each game

Set-Up
Remove questions from booklet, cut out individual questions, and stack them face-down into five piles, one for each category. The rules of play are based on three individual players, but three teams, comprised of three or fewer players each, may compete against one another. If teams are used, each player within a team takes a turn for the team by rolling the die and answering a question. Each player within a team must take a turn in the designated order of play. Teammates are **not** allowed to assist the person answering a question.

Object of the Game
The winner is the player that first lands in the center logo and correctly answers a question from category 5. Before answering a game-winning question, a player must land in each of the five categories and correctly answer a question.

How to Play
Each player selects a marker and places it in one of the three circular starting spaces. Three players compete in each game. The player whose birthday comes earliest in the year goes first; year of birth is not considered. The birthday order also determines the order of play for the other players.

The player with the first turn rolls the die and moves the marker the indicated number of spaces in any direction. A player may not combine forward and backward moves for one roll of the die. A marker cannot rest on a space that is already occupied, although it can pass over another marker.

Each space on the board has a number except for the circular starting spaces, which are free turn spaces. The number on the

---

[1] Developed from the "Drexel Accounting Trivia Game," designed in 1989 by William A. Stahlin, Drexel University.

space determines the category of question that will be asked. There are five categories:

1. **All about Assets and Everything about Expenses**
2. **Learning Liabilities and Reviewing Revenues**
3. **Figuring Financials**
4. **Managing Managerial**
5. **Sundry Subjects**

The questioner is the player to the left of the player taking the turn. The questioner selects a question from the proper category pile and clearly asks the player with the turn to answer. A player may ask to have the questioned repeated only once.

If the player taking the turn gives the correct answer without consultation, then play continues. If a player answers incorrectly or takes longer than 15 seconds to respond, the turn ends and play passes to the next player. The player who misses must wait for another turn to roll and attempt another category.

When a category requirement is met, the player checks the score sheet. Sometimes a player will land on a category after the requirement has been met. The player must answer another question from the category in order to continue the turn. Once questions from all five categories have been answered correctly, the player may proceed up any ladder to the center of the board. A player can reach the center only on an exact roll of the die. If a player cannot advance, the turn passes. When the roll exactly places the marker in the center logo, a player must correctly answer a question from category 5 in order to win. If the question is answered incorrectly, the turn ends, and the player must leave the center on the next turn, returning to the center only by another exact roll of the die.

Because a player can continue a turn by answering correctly, a win is possible on the first turn. If this happens, any other player who has not yet had a turn is allowed a chance to duplicate the feat and create a tie.

ANY GAME DECISIONS (SUCH AS RULES, ACCEPTABILITY OF ANSWERS, DISPUTES, ETC.) NOT COVERED BY THESE RULES SHOULD BE RESOLVED FAIRLY BY ALL PLAYERS. IF SATISFACTORY SETTLEMENT IS NOT READILY ACHIEVED FOR ALL PLAYERS, THE PLAYER TAKING THE TURN WHEN THE DISAGREEMENT AROSE SHOULD RE-ROLL THE DIE AND RESTART THE TURN FROM THE PRIOR POSITION.

Good luck and have fun!

West Accounting Trivia Scoresheet

Date _____

NAMES OF PLAYERS

TEAM 1	TEAM 2	TEAM 3

SCORING

CATEGORIES	TEAM 1	TEAM 2	TEAM 3
1. All about Assets and Everything about Expenses			
2. Learning Liabilities and Reviewing Revenues			
3. Figuring Financials			
4. Managing Managerial			
5. Sundry Subjects			

Category 1: All about Assets and Everything about Expenses

If a calendar-year company paid $600 for an insurance premium on September 1, what should be the balance in the related asset account at the end of the year?

A: $400 ($600/12 × 8 months).

Name three examples of intangible assets.

A: Three of the following: franchises, patents, copyrights, trademarks, product formulas, or goodwill.

Of the following items, which would not be classified in the cash account on the balance sheet: coins, checks, 6-month certificates of deposit, money orders, or IOUs from employees?

A: 6-month certificates of deposit (short-term investment) and IOUs from employees (receivable).

What is the effect of a bank credit memo on a depositor's account balance?

A: A bank credit memo increases the cash balance of a depositor.

Name the two criteria that must be met to classify a short-term investment as a current asset.

A: (1) readily salable and (2) intended to be converted into cash within the operating cycle or one year, whichever is longer.

At what point do expenditures from a petty cash fund get recorded as expenses?

A: Journal entries for the petty cash disbursements are made when the fund is replenished.

A deposit in transit is reported on a bank reconciliation as an addition to the ending balance of the _____?

A: Bank.

If a company uses the allowance method of accounting for uncollectibles, what impact does the write-off of an uncollectible customer account have on the firm's net income?

A: None. (The allowance account is debited and the receivable account is credited.)

Category 1	**Category 1**
Category 1	**Category 1**
Category 1	**Category 1**
Category 1	**Category 1**

If a company uses the allowance method of accounting for uncollectibles, what impact does the write-off of an uncollectible customer account have on the firm's net accounts receivable balance?

A: None. (The allowance account is debited and the receivable account is credited.)

If a company was primarily concerned with the principle of matching, which method of estimating uncollectible accounts would likely be used?

A: The income statement approach, where uncollectibles are estimated on the basis of total sales or credit sales.

What is the inventory cost flow assumption in which the oldest costs incurred become part of cost of goods sold?

A: FIFO.

Which of the following would not be included in Parker's cost of ending inventory: work in process in Parker's factory; inventories held for a consignee; goods in transit to a customer, shipping terms F.O.B. shipping point; and finished goods awaiting shipment to customers?

A: Inventories held for a consignee and goods in transit to a customer, shipped F.O.B. shipping point.

At the end of an accounting period, goods available for sale is segregated into two different cost categories. What are they?

A: Ending inventory and cost of goods sold.

In a period of rising prices, which inventory valuation method tends to result in the highest income taxes?

A: FIFO.

What is the major reason that land is not depreciated?

A: The major reason is that land does not have a limited life and is considered to provide indefinite benefits.

Which of the following items is not included in the cost of an asset: purchase price, freight charges, insurance during transit, installation costs, medical cost of injured installer, special electrical wiring, and costs of trial runs?

A: The medical costs of an injured installer.

Category 1	Category 1
Category 1	Category 1
Category 1	Category 1
Category 1	Category 1

Explain the proper treatment of interest costs related to the *purchase* of a new building.

A: Interest costs related to the purchase of a new building should be charged to expense as incurred.

Define the term *depreciable base*.

A: Asset cost minus residual value (or the total amount that will be written off to depreciation expense over the asset's life).

At the beginning of the current year, a company acquired a patent for $68,000. The patent had an original legal life of 17 years at the date of issuance. Only four of the 17 years remained when acquired. What would be the amount of amortization for the current year?

A: $17,000 ($68,000/4 years).

Will amortization of a bond premium result in a corporation's interest expense being less than or greater than the interest paid?

A: Less than.

When the percentage ownership of an investee corporation is less than 20% of the outstanding voting stock and no significant investor influence is present, the accounting method to be used is what?

A: Cost, subject to lower of cost or market considerations.

What are the three most common "quick" assets?

A: (1) Cash, (2) short-term investments, and (3) accounts receivable.

In evaluating the acqusition of long-term assets, which of the following three methods does not consider the time value of money: internal rate of return, the payback method, or the net-present-value method?

A: The payback method.

What do you call an exclusive right to use specific brand names and symbols for a period of 10 years, with renewal possible if certain conditions are met?

A: Trademark.

Category 1	Category 1
Category 1	Category 1
Category 1	Category 1
Category 1	Category 1

Category 2: Learning Liabilities and Reviewing Revenues

In reviewing the records of Phillips Company, you discover that three months' rent of $750 was prepaid to Griffith Realty on November 1. What account and amount would be shown on Griffith's November 30 balance sheet?

A: Unearned rental revenue, $500.

Where does the payee's contingent liability appear in the financial statements when a note receivable has been discounted at a bank?

A: The contingent liability for a discounted note is typically disclosed in a note to the financial statements.

How are gains on exchanges of similar assets handled for accounting purposes?

A: They are deducted from the cost basis of the newly acquired asset.

How would a gain on the sale of an asset be calculated?

A: By comparing the proceeds received on the sale to the asset's book value (cost minus accumulated depreciation).

What kind of account is "discount on notes payable?"

A: Contra liability.

What are two guidelines that must be met in order for a contingent liability to be recorded in the accounts?

A: (1) It is probable that the future event will occur and (2) the amount of the liability can be reasonably estimated.

Name the payroll taxes that are incurred by an employer.

A: Social security/Medicare, federal unemployment, and state unemployment.

Name three different situations where a business collects monies from customers and employees and reports such amounts as current liabilities.

A: Sales tax collected from customers; customer prepayment of such items as service contracts and season tickets; and payroll withholdings for taxes, union dues, and employee contributions.

Category 2	**Category 2**
Category 2	**Category 2**
Category 2	**Category 2**
Category 2	**Category 2**

Revenue is said to be realized when two tests are met. What are these two tests?

A: (1) The earnings process is complete or virtually complete, and (2) the amount of revenue can be objectively measured.

Give an example of when it is permissible to recognize revenue during the production process.

A: The percentage-of-completion method reports revenue ratably over the life of a construction project.

Warner Developers has extreme difficulty in estimating future construction costs. What method of accounting for revenues would the company likely use in relation to a three-year highway project?

A: Completed-contract method.

Give an example of when it is permissible to recognize revenue at the time of a cash receipt involving only a partial payment by the customer.

A: Installment method of accounting.

How are liquidation gains in partnership divided among the partners?

A: According to the partnership's profit-and-loss-sharing ratio.

Are dividends in arrears on cumulative preferred stock a liability?

A: No.

Bates, Inc. recently issued $400,000 of 10 percent bonds at 102. Is the effective interest rate equal to, greater than, or less than the contract interest rate?

A: Less than.

When bonds are sold at a discount, will the carrying value be higher or lower than the face value?

A: Lower.

Category 2

Category 2

Category 2

Category 2

Category 2

Category 2

Category 2

Category 2

When bonds are issued between interest payment dates, will the amount of cash paid to the bond holder on the next interest payment date be higher, lower, or the same as the amount of cash that would have been paid if the bonds had not been issued between interest payment dates?

A: The same (but part of the cash will be a repayment for the amount collected for interest when the bonds were issued).

Will annual bond interest revenue be higher, lower, or the same as the cash received for a bondholder's investment, if the bonds were purchased at a premium?

A: Lower.

If a corporation repurchases its outstanding bonds for less than their carrying value, will a gain or loss result?

A: A gain.

What do you call an agreement between a company and its employees that provides for retirement benefits?

A: A pension plan.

A long-term note issued to finance the purchase of real estate is called a

_____.

A: Mortgage.

Define gross profit.

A: Net sales minus cost of goods sold.

Suppose that a company uses special journals to record its daily transactions. In which journal would cash sales be recorded?

A: Cash receipts journal.

On which financial statement would you find exchange gains from foreign currency transactions?

A: The income statement.

Category 2	**Category 2**
Category 2	**Category 2**
Category 2	**Category 2**
Category 2	**Category 2**

Category 3: Figuring Financials

Of the income statement, balance sheet, or statement of owner's equity, which covers a specific point in time as opposed to a period of time?

A: Balance sheet.

If Amanda Fitz accidentally debited an expense account rather than an asset account, what would be the effect on net income?

A: Understated.

On which financial statement would unearned service revenue appear?

A: Balance sheet.

How should current assets be organized on the balance sheet?

A: In order of their liquidity.

Where are gains and losses normally reported on a multiple-step income statement?

A: In the "other revenue and expense" category.

How is the cash short and over account classified in the financial statements?

A: The balance in the account is reported on the income statement with other miscellaneous expense and revenue items.

Blackford's Books is a retail store. What is the chief financial reason for using the retail method of estimating its inventory?

A: Interim financial statements prepared between physical counts.

Is the disclosure of inflation-adjusted financial information mandatory or voluntary?

A: Voluntary.

Category 3

Category 3

Category 3

Category 3

Category 3

Category 3

Category 3

Category 3

On which financial statement would you find partners' salaries?

A: Statement of partners' equity.

On an income statement, explain where freight-in and freight-out would appear.

A: Freight-in appears as part of the net purchases computation within the cost-of-goods-sold section of the income statement. Freight-out is regarded as a selling cost and is listed among a company's business expenses.

If a company adopts the net method of accounting for purchases, which new account may appear on the income statement?

A: Purchases discounts lost.

If a corporation has assets of $100,000, liabilities of $10,000, total capital stock of $40,000, and total investments by stockholders of $50,000, what must retained earnings be?

A: $40,000 ($100,000 − $10,000 − $50,000).

If a corporation's total stockholders' equity is $1,000,000, and it has 100,000 shares of common stock authorized and 50,000 shares issued and outstanding, what is the book value per share?

A: $20 ($1,000,000/50,000).

On which financial statement would you find "gains" from treasury stock sales reported?

A: On the balance sheet, as part of the stockholders' equity.

Exactly where on the income statement would you find the financial results of discontinued operations?

A: In a separate category immediately following income from continuing operations.

On which financial statement would you look for prior period adjustments?

A: Statement of retained earnings.

Category 3	Category 3
Category 3	Category 3
Category 3	Category 3
Category 3	Category 3

What two criteria must be satisfied for an event to be classified as an extraordinary item?

A: (1) Unusual in nature and (2) infrequent in occurrence.

When one company acquires a controlling interest in another business, the firms have, in substance, become a single affiliated economic unit. What kind of financial statements would be issued as a result?

A: Consolidated financial statements.

On a statement of cash flows, in which section would you find payment of corporate dividends?

A: Financing activities.

What are the two alternate methods that can be used in preparing the operating section of a statement of cash flows?

A: The direct method and the indirect method.

In which section of a statement of cash flows would you find the cash purchase of inventory?

A: Operating activities.

A corporation had a current ratio of 4 at the end of a month, just before paying $1,000 of accounts payable with cash. As a result of this payment, will the current ratio increase, decrease, or remained unchanged?

A: Increase.

What do you call the ratio derived by dividing net credit sales by average accounts receivable?

A: Accounts receivable turnover.

Would a company rather obtain a qualified opinion or an unqualified opinion from its auditor?

A: Unqualified.

Category 3	Category 3
Category 3	Category 3
Category 3	Category 3
Category 3	Category 3

Which of the following items is properly classified as factory overhead: wages of a carpenter who custom builds furniture, cost of sandpaper used in the production of furniture, or depreciation on office equipment used at company headquarters?

A: Cost of sandpaper used in the production of furniture.

Which of the following is an example of a variable cost: salary of a plant supervisor, advertising costs, direct materials, or straight-line depreciation on a factory machine?

A: Direct materials.

What agency established the "ground rules" for managerial accounting practices?

A: No specific entity exists to formulate the ground rules for managerial accounting practices.

What are the three cost elements of a manufactured product?

A: Direct materials, direct labor, and factory overhead.

When will a product cost appear on an income statement?

A: When the item (i.e., good) to which the cost has been attached is sold and becomes part of cost of goods sold.

What two elements make up conversion cost?

A: Direct labor plus factory overhead.

What element is missing from the following equation: cost of goods manufactured = direct materials used + direct labor + beginning work in process – ending work in process?

A: Factory overhead.

What are the two components of prime cost?

A: Direct materials plus direct labor.

Category 4	Category 4
Category 4	**Category 4**
Category 4	**Category 4**
Category 4	**Category 4**

Which of the following businesses would be least likely to use a job costing system: an automobile repair shop, a custom home builder, a crude oil refinery, or a motion picture producer?

A: Crude oil refinery.

The journal entry to record the use of indirect materials in production activities involves a debit to which account?

A: Factory overhead.

In deriving an overhead application rate, what is the numerator?

A: Estimated factory overhead.

If overhead is overapplied, will the factory overhead account contain a debit or credit balance?

A: A credit balance.

If 100,000 units were started and finished during the first month of a company's operations and 80,000 units were 25 percent complete at the end of the month, how many equivalent units were produced during the month?

A: 120,000   [100,000 + .25(80,000)].

Companies that use a process costing system document the period's manufacturing activity on a _____.

A: Production cost report.

In managerial accounting, what does ABC stand for?

A: Activity-based costing.

What do you call a production system in which inventory levels are ideally zero?

A: Just-in-time.

Category 4	Category 4
Category 4	Category 4
Category 4	Category 4
Category 4	Category 4

Patter Company has sales of $1,000,000, variable costs that total 75 percent of sales, and fixed costs of $200,000. What is the firm's break-even point?

A: $800,000 (S = .75S + $200,000).

What do you call the area of activity where a cost relationship is expected to hold true so that break-even analysis can be performed?

A: The relevant range.

Of the following budgets, which is normally the first to be prepared: the production budget, sales budget, or cash budget?

A: The sales budget.

The difference between the actual factory overhead incurred during the period and the overhead budgeted for the actual hours worked is known as the _____ variance.

A: Overhead spending variance.

What do you call a reporting system based on the organizational structure of a firm, where managers of each segment are held accountable for operating results?

A: Responsibility accounting.

The difference between the actual and standard prices, multiplied by the actual quantity of materials purchased and put into production, is called the _____ variance.

A: Material price variance.

Are favorable variances recorded in the accounts as debits or credits?

A: Credits.

Which costing method is the acceptable method for external reporting of product costs—absorption costing or direct costing?

A: Absorption costing.

Category 4	Category 4
Category 4	Category 4
Category 4	Category 4
Category 4	Category 4

Category 5: Sundry Subjects

What is the name of the assumption that holds that a business must be viewed as a unit that is separate from its owners?

A: Entity.

A $350 debit to cash was accidentally posted as a credit to accounts payable. In a trial balance, what will be the difference between the debit and credit totals?

A: $700.

If you find a credit to income summary in the final step in closing, did the business have a profit or loss for the period?

A: Loss.

Which balance sheet account will not appear on a company's post-closing trial balance?

A: The drawing account (or the dividend account, in the case of a corporation).

In terms of a business, which is generally preferable: a long or a short operating cycle?

A: A short operating cycle is preferable, so that funds will be available more quickly.

Consider the four accounts: purchases, purchases discounts, purchases discounts lost, and purchases returns and allowances. Which of these would not be used in a company employing the net method of recording purchases?

A: Purchases discounts.

If you are the purchasing agent for a business, would you prefer to buy goods with the terms F.O.B shipping point or F.O.B. destination?

A: F.O.B. destination, because the seller would be responsible for the freight charges.

What is a control account and where is it found?

A: A control account, found in the general ledger, is an account comprised of numerous lower-level (or "sub") accounts.

Category 5

Category 5

Category 5

Category 5

Category 5

Category 5

Category 5

Category 5

What are two accounting functions that should be separated because of lack of compatibility?

A: Two of the following: transaction authorization, transaction recording, and asset custody.

What is the ultimate guideline that should be used to decide the specific controls to build into an accounting system?

A: Cost-benefit. Controls should be implemented if the benefits of use exceed the costs of implementation and operation.

Because of a mathematical error, the 19X7 ending inventory included goods at a $5,000 figure when the goods had actually cost $500. What would be the effect on 19X8 net income as a result of this error?

A: 19X8 net income would be understated.

What is the major reason that the perpetual inventory system has increased in popularity in recent years?

A: Computers and state-of-the-art information systems have reduced the tedium associated with the perpetual method and have made its benefits available at a reduced overall cost.

What is the accounting principle that allows some long-lived items of property, plant, and equipment to be expensed when their benefits will in fact last over many periods?

A: Materiality.

What does MACRS stand for?

A: Modified accelerated cost recovery system.

What would be the denominator of the fraction used in the sum-of-the-years'-digits method of depreciation when the useful life of an asset is estimated to be 11 years?

A: 66 $[(11 \times 12)/2]$.

Which organization has ultimate authority over the reporting practices of most large corporations?

A: The Securities Exchange Commission (SEC).

Category 5

Category 5

Category 5

Category 5

Category 5

Category 5

Category 5

Category 5

Metro Delivery was founded in 19X1 and implemented a straight-line depreciation policy for its truck fleet. From the viewpoint of a statement user, should Metro use straight-line depreciation in 19X2 and 19X3?

A: Yes, because the use of the same accounting practices from period to period promotes the consistency principle.

Name the principle that holds that an entity must provide a complete reporting of the facts important enough to influence the judgment of an informed financial statement user.

A: Disclosure.

Name two organizations that have been established to help develop international accounting standards.

A: The International Accounting Standards Committee and the International Federation of Accountants.

A partner bought a parcel of land several years ago at a cost of $50,000. She invested it in her partnership when the market value was estimated to be $75,000. The partnership plans to sell the land in two years when the land should be worth $90,000. At what amount should the partnership record land invested by the partner?

A: $75,000, the land's fair market value at the time of investment.

What is the term that describes the ability of each partner to act as an agent of the partnership in business transactions?

A: Mutual agency.

What is the term that means the legal life of a partnership has ended, even if business is not discontinued?

A: Dissolution.

If stock is issued in exchange for services, at what amount should the transaction be recorded?

A: The fair market value of the services or the fair market value of the stock, whichever is more clearly determinable.

What is the term that means the issuing corporation retains the right to reacquire its stock at a preset price?

A: Callable.

Category 5	Category 5
Category 5	Category 5
Category 5	Category 5
Category 5	Category 5

What two conditions must be satisfied to declare and distribute a cash dividend?

A: (1) Adequate cash balance and (2) adequate balance in retained earnings.

Does a corporation become legally liable for dividend distributions on the date of declaration or the date of record?

A: Date of declaration.

Is a dollar received today worth more or less than a $1 received one year from today?

A: A dollar today is worth more than a dollar in the future.

Define net sales.

A: Gross sales reduced by sales discounts and sales returns and allowances.

Computer software that resembles a huge columnar work sheet and is useful in a variety of accounting applications is generally known as _____.

A: An electronic spreadsheet.

What is the due date of a 60-day note dated May 1?

A: June 30.

Using the generally accepted accounting method, what account will be debited when an uncollectible account is written off?

A: Allowance for uncollectible accounts.

Name the process of taking a future amount and bringing it back to its value today.

A: Discounting.

Category 5	Category 5
Category 5	Category 5
Category 5	Category 5
Category 5	Category 5

Creekside, Inc. began business at the beginning of the current year. The company produced 42,000 units, but sold only 35,000 by the end of the year. Would direct costing net income be higher or lower than absorption costing net income?

A: Lower.

Tad's Limited has idle capacity and is studying whether to accept a special order for 1,000 units of its sole product. The product usually sells for $20 and has related variable and fixed manufacturing costs of $12 and $4, respectively. If the special order is accepted at a price of $15 per unit, Tad's overall profitability will increase by _____.

A: $3,000   [1,000 × ($15 − $12)].

All other things being equal, does a company normally prefer to have a high or low inventory turnover?

A: High.

Where in an annual report would you find a summary of significant accounting policies?

A: Notes to the financial statements.

What is the term used to describe a company's net income divided by the weighted-average number of common shares?

A: Earnings per share.

Which of the following is rarely a consideration when analyzing a long-term project: the cost of the investment, the lowest rate of return acceptable to management, or the company's current ratio?

A: The company's current ratio.

When several items of property, plant, and equipment are acquired in a lump-sum purchase, should the purchase price be apportioned among the assets (1) in an equal distribution; (2) according to the individual appraised values of the assets; or (3) as a proportion of their original list prices?

A: According to the individual appraised values of the assets.

Is the following statement true or false: special journals eliminate the need for a general journal?

A: False.

Category 5	Category 5
Category 5	Category 5
Category 5	Category 5
Category 5	Category 5